THE PRACTITIONER INQUIRY SERIES

Marilyn Cochran-Smith and Susan L. Lytle, Series Editors

ADVISORY BOARD: JoBeth Allen, Judy Buchanan, Curt Dudley-Marling, Robert Fecho,
Sarah Freedman, Dixie Goswami, Joyce E. King, Sarah Michaels, Luis Moll,
Susan Noffke, Sharon Ravitch, Marty Rutherford, Lynne Strieb, Diane Waff, Ken Zeichner

TEACHING
IN
Themes

An Approach to Schoolwide Learning, Creating Community, and Differentiating Instruction

EDITED BY

Deborah Meier
Matthew Knoester
Katherine Clunis D'Andrea

TEACHERS COLLEGE PRESS

TEACHERS COLLEGE | COLUMBIA UNIVERSITY

NEW YORK AND LONDON

Published by Teachers College Press, 1234 Amsterdam Avenue, New York, NY 10027

Library of Congress Cataloging-in-Publication Data

Teaching in themes : an approach to schoolwide learning, creating community, and
    differentiating instruction / edited by Deborah Meier, Matthew Knoester, Katherine
    Clunis D'Andrea.
        pages cm
    Includes bibliographical references and index.
    ISBN 978-0-8077-5699-7 (pbk. : alk. paper) —
    ISBN 978-0-8077-5700-0 (hardcover : alk. paper) —
    ISBN 978-0-8077-7411-3 (ebook)
        1. Mission Hill School (Boston, Mass.) 2. Public schools—Massachusetts—Boston.
    3. School environment—Massachusetts—Boston. I. Meier, Deborah, editor of
    compilation.
    LD7501.B22T43 2015
    371.0109744'61—dc23   2015016233

ISBN 978-0-8077-5699-7 (paper)
ISBN 978-0-8077-5700-0 (hardcover)
ISBN 978-0-8077-7411-3 (ebook)

Printed on acid-free paper
Manufactured in the United States of America

22 21 20 19 18 17 16 15   8 7 6 5 4 3 2 1

Dedicated to Eleanor Duckworth, Brenda Engel, and to the late Vito Perrone and Ted Sizer—all inspiring educators who helped to make Mission Hill School possible

Contents

Preface

I used to say, "It doesn't matter what you study, just how you study it." I still suspect that's true. Still, isn't there some subject matter that opens the door more widely to both the best of pedagogy and the best of knowledge about the world? Aren't some things more important than others? Aren't some topics easier to investigate in ways that are compatible with developing strong intellectual habits?

The accounts in this book were influenced by the 30-plus years of experience I brought into the proposal to start Mission Hill. I'm still not sure where I stand, although I'm sure of what I stand against! And an imposed state or federal curriculum is definitely on my hit list, even if it goes by the name of standards.

In fact, I liked the idea, as posed by Ted Sizer, of standards as a flag held high, not a script laid down. But the power of the standards he proposed was that they'd require the school itself to articulate and assess them—they had to be in the hands of those who implemented them and judged their efficacy. They require frequent revision as we learn from them. The flag we honored in 1776 (or whenever) did not stand for the same set of values and priorities that it did a hundred or two hundred years later. The kind of republic then envisioned had a narrow base—men with property. Today, sometimes begrudgingly, we accept a definition that includes men without property, women with and without, and people of all colors and races and languages. On the other hand, we're more confused about when and how "foreigners" can become citizens than we were 250 years ago. Odd, isn't it?

I started out in education visiting classrooms throughout Chicago's mostly segregated South Side K–8 schools. I visited in the guise of a substitute teacher. While I had my credentials, I entered such assignments with astonished ignorance. I was more or less chased out of one school, having decided that, given my inability to control the class, they'd be safer without me. I had my good days. But my students for sure learned less than I did. This job was a part-time vocation, while my full-time one was divided between raising three children and working with the Congress of Racial Equality.

But the experience of applying to be a sub and the way I was treated in school and after school, by both the adults and the students, was eye-opening. How 12 years of such a demeaning school culture might affect the kind of relationship an 18-year-old graduate had to society—the "public"—seemed far from imbued with hope. For me at the time, curriculum seemed for the moment less relevant than the culture of the school, the ways in which everyone—adults and children—was treated.

In an odd way, it was teaching kindergarten that got me interested in the "curriculum"—how the setting of the classroom and the interests of the children could be both a curriculum and a management tool. I rediscovered the obvious fact that interested human beings—of all ages—are the most efficiently productive learners, focused and perseverant when their curiosity is aroused. I found out, also, that traditional early childhood interests are hardly a mystery—they are the fundamental "stuff" of the world—sand, clay, paint, water, animals, plants, art, and each other. I saw that using these in early childhood education is all it takes, plus exploring the world outside the classroom with all its entrancing objects: elevators, escalators, tall buildings, bridges, trees, flowers, stores, cars, trains, subways, and on and on.

For the next nearly 10 years, I grew fascinated by the ordinary, both objects and words, and of course living things (how fascinating insects were for me and the children). These were the components of a curriculum, and this kind of curriculum had a name: *emergent*. The curriculum emerges from children's interests—the questions they ask explicitly as well as those that we can observe in action. This process wasn't dampened by having themes—a more focused core, which made it perhaps more manageable for a teacher and encouraged more cross-dialogue. Themes didn't seem to dampen the spirit of discovery as long as we didn't take it too seriously.

There were trade-offs. I turned Chicago's kindergarten curriculum upside down; that year was supposed to be about "the ways in which Los Angeles and Tokyo are much alike," and we spent time instead looking at how Chicago and Tokyo differed. It caused a small stir when an inspector actually appeared from the Chicago Public Schools central office to see if I was complying. My principal that year was a charming man of Japanese descent, and he was delighted at my sabotage, so I learned the teacher trick of apologizing and ignoring—for both good and bad, I suppose.

I liked the idea of whole-school themes because it created a lot for teachers to learn about together, as well as many examples of ways in which a topic could be studied. It made it easy to have older kids join younger ones, the older ones adding their sophistication in ways that were less intrusive than my own at times. In the school's returning to the same subject every 4 years, such growing sophistication was honored, as was an understanding of how much more there always was to learn.

So it's not necessary to note that the ideas behind E. D. Hirsch's core curriculum as well as both the pedagogical and curricular "standards" of the Common Core didn't fit our approach. Not only were they often in conflict with basic knowledge on child development and likely to damage deviant learners, but they threatened to lessen the focus on children as fascinating learners that made teaching fun and worthwhile. The whole concept was part and parcel of an effort to make nationwide testing easier, and thus make it easier to compare children with each other across classrooms, schools, cities, and states, and, ideally, compare learners in the United States with those of all our international competitors.

Fitting everything in from birth to age 18 was simple enough: Just design backward (an idea that has, alas, been interpreted in ways that assume we can know exactly how things will turn out); document carefully; and test often. The process rested on checklists of "to-dos" for teachers and watching alertly for where each child was falling behind. Over time it would increase the use of technology to gauge the pace of children's learning and would entail the removal of lively interactions between people and between people and the stuff of the world as each child entered his or her own learning box. Of course, the plan was unlikely to play out quite so smoothly, as both teachers and children were inescapably human, unique, peculiar, and ornery. But it was likely to damage precisely those aspects of our humanity that we almost universally agreed were so vital to the future of humankind—aspects such as empathy, curiosity, drive, self-regulation (a term I've recently discovered), perseverance, and the ability to discover novelty!

We shall overcome this too, and fortunately at Mission Hill, the "old-fashioned" way is still thriving as we sneak around all the latest bad ideas. It probably doesn't help our test scores K–8, but so far it hasn't hurt our graduates' ability to pass the Massachusetts-mandated graduation tests. We're keeping our fingers crossed and hoping the whole phenomenon will pass before we too get swept into a new dead end.

—Deborah W. Meier, Hillsdale, New York

Acknowledgments

The authors would like to thank the following people for their support of this work: Leigh Bailey, Ron Berger, Julie Bowes, John Bylander, Janet Carvalho, Sam Chaltain, Marilyn Cochran-Smith, Dani Coleman, Latisha Coleman, Marija Crosson, Larry Cuban, Alessandro D'Andrea, Antonino D'Andrea, Nyla D'Andrea, Linda Darling-Hammond, Brian Ellerbeck, Brenda Engel, Helen Featherstone, Jay Featherstone, Abby Foley, Dominic Gates, Kyle Gates, Barbara Henriquez, Alain Jehlen, Barbara Jones, Quela Jules, Amber Keizer, Alfie Kohn, Morgan Krieger, Diane Levin, Susan Lytle, Mike McLaughlin, Deborah Meier, Amina Michel-Lord, Monty Neill, Scott Nine, Dennis Powell, Emily Renwick, Anna Schoup, Keja Valens, Carrie Vance, Jubilee Knoester Vance, Nicolaus Knoester Vance, Erin Williams, Rosemary Williams, and the entire staff of Mission Hill School.

CHAPTER 1

Introduction

Deborah Meier
Matthew Knoester
Katherine Clunis D'Andrea

Schools are institutions where hundreds, sometimes thousands, of children and adults come together for the purpose of educating students. But how often do these institutions feel like communities of learners? How can teachers and schools create meaningful communal and individual learning experiences when students come with widely differing skills, abilities, experiences, and sensitivities? How can teachers authentically assess the learning of their students and build on students' strengths and interests in ways that enrich the larger community? Given the history of classrooms as closed, and even secret, boxes that create an institution called school, how can schools be turned into places where all participants—teachers and students—are learning from each other? These are the big questions that guide much of the work of teachers at the Mission Hill School in Boston and that are addressed in depth in the chapters of this book.

The Mission Hill School is a small K–8 public pilot school in the Boston Public Schools system founded by Deborah Meier and colleagues in 1997. There are many unique features about the Mission Hill School that warrant the large amount of attention it has received in books, articles, and a popular new film series. It is small, culturally diverse, democratically governed, and dedicated to education for democratic citizenship. It uses portfolios of student work for assessment, and its graduates have been shown to achieve academic success in high school and college. The school saw its mission from the beginning as creating a setting—a whole schoolwide community, including parents and teachers alongside students, with all their differences and diversities (individual, social, class, and racial/ethnic)—as a strength and not a dilemma. Just as each teacher sought to create a classroom of strong, differentiated students, each functioning as an independent and confident learner, he or she also sought to create a community of learners, and so too did the school aim for such a goal schoolwide. The teachers at Mission Hill School have thought outside the box of traditional schooling to answer the questions we posed above. The school has several unusual features that serve to aid in addressing these questions.

One unique feature of the school that has received little attention is the school's approach to curriculum, which involves 3-month whole-school thematic units. Each year, the entire school (with partial exception of the middle school) explores three broad thematic units together. One unit focuses on a particular aspect of U.S. history, another on an ancient civilization, and a third on a major area of science. These broad themes allow students to experience a sense of immersion in a world of inquiry, and allow teachers and students to design and plan together smaller emergent inquiries in their own classrooms within these themes. The teachers at the school are able to share information and resources, including guest speakers, musicians, artifacts, field trips, and books. The power of aesthetics plays a key role in this work. The faculty at the Mission Hill School realizes that the aesthetic value of student work can have a transformational effect on the identities of students. For this reason, many of the projects and activities completed by students within long-duration thematic units undergo multiple revisions, along with peer and adult critique within a noncompetitive and supportive environment. Projects are designed by teachers and students to be eventually presentable before audiences of peers, parents, and members of the community.

The detailed descriptions of the thematic units found in this book and the answers to the framing questions above are addressed not only to an audience of like-minded teachers who teach at small public progressive schools like the Mission Hill School. Rather, we know that teachers in all settings face these questions. Teachers never work with a truly homogeneous group of students who equally thrive on just one set of activities. Rather, teachers must continually differentiate their instruction, thinking about the needs of each individual child, if teachers are to support the learning and growth of the whole range of students. As Tomlinson and McTighe (2006) remind us, "Few teachers find their work effective or satisfying when they 'serve up' a curriculum—even an elegant one—to their students with no regard for their varied learning needs" (p. 1).

We argue that designing 3-month-long whole-school thematic units is a powerful approach to addressing the framing questions above. To avoid misunderstanding, we wish to clarify a few key terms that we use at the Mission Hill School and that are found in this book, starting with *differentiated instruction*. "Differentiated" can mean or suggest some catch phrase for continually updating what each student has completed or understands on a standardized curriculum or set of skills in chronological order. But for us, differentiating is led mostly by teachers following students' leads, observing closely, and bringing in the "just right" book, experiment, or material. And "instruction" often implies a teacher instructing—explicitly teaching. This may sometimes be useful and other times not. At Mission

Hill School, students' curiosity is highly valued and is seen as the driving force for much of the learning that takes place, so the instruction that happens is often in the form of the teacher as coach, providing materials and provocative questions and experiences for students while encouraging students to make key decisions about their own learning.

Thematic curriculum is interdisciplinary subject exploration whose components are bound together by a large overarching theme. At the Mission Hill School, there is generally a large theme that the whole school explores together, and individual teachers and classes may focus on smaller subthemes within their classes based on considerations of age appropriateness as well as student and teacher interests. For example, the whole school might be exploring natural science, but individual teachers might focus more specifically on the human body or the life cycles of various animals, insects, or plant life. And even within these subthemes, individual students might be working on exploring a specific aspect of the human body or of the life cycle of a particular species.

Emergent curriculum refers to the individual interests of students within a classroom that the teacher encourages, allowing time for a student to explore a particular question or topic, providing resources that enrich the exploration. For instance, one year at Mission Hill School the yard behind the school became inundated with snails. They were everywhere! The students were fascinated by these creatures, generating hundreds of questions about them and collecting them to study more closely. Several teachers decided to use this opportunity to turn this accidental happening into a major exercise in an emergent curriculum. The students and staff began to conduct research into why these snails were there, the biology of snails, and more. Artwork was created, and ecosystems were designed to provide the snails with indoor habitats. The richness of the snail curriculum resided in the immediate accessibility of the subject matter for all students. It provided experiential and hands-on learning opportunities for all students, not differentially more for those who had different prior experiences with snails. Further, the topic of "snails" was one that could be investigated by children at different ability levels—from the most sophisticated scientist with deep background knowledge to the student who had never explored the complexity of snails from a scientific, artistic, or literary perspective. Teachers at Mission Hill School are forever seeking a balance between deductively choosing a broad topic to explore as a school or class that allows shared resources and adequate planning time for teachers and the more inductive or emergent approach, which builds on the immediate interests and curiosities of students and generally provides the most powerful motivation for students to seriously explore and play with new ideas.

Integrated curriculum is an approach to teaching that weaves disciplinary knowledge from various subjects together to allow students to be at the center of the decisionmaking process. This approach is characterized

by lengthy, uninterrupted periods of time during which students are working on various long-term projects. Students are generally allowed to move
around the classroom and school, acquiring materials, solving problems,
and reading and writing, and the whole class will come together for limited
amounts of time to plan work periods, share explorations, and teach or
hear mini-lessons.

We are not arguing that the thematic approach described in this book
represents a utopian vision. Clearly, trade-offs have to be made. By valu-
ing thematic, emergent, and integrated curricula we are taking a depth-
over-breadth approach, one that necessarily means that some curricular
topics—including topics that individuals may argue are critically important—remain largely unstudied by graduates of the Mission Hill School.
By rotating planned curricular themes, we attempt to ensure balance and
exposure to a range of important disciplinary topics (see Appendix A for a
list of themes). Through the repetition of themes every 4 years, students
also have an opportunity to return to an old theme with gained knowledge about the subject and greater sophistication. We believe that the
trade-offs are worth it. The deep-immersion approach challenges students
to think critically and more like scientists when studying science, for example, as they see much more of why a particular topic fascinates scientists
and as they note the space between problems and mysteries—those areas
where professionals work to solve real problems of inquiry. The thematic
units also encourage collaboration for both students and teachers. Teachers across the grades can do planning together, arrange joint class trips,
gather and share rich resources, and give their students opportunities to
display work and present performances to one another. Thematic units
allow time for students to play with materials and create impressive and
artistic projects or solve complex problems, with help from other older
or younger students. Once again, this approach creates a sense of schoolwide community, classroom pride, and opportunities for each individual
or small group to "show off" to an appreciative audience.

We also do not want to give the false impression that these approaches
were invented by teachers at the Mission Hill School. In Chapter 2, the
founding principal of the school, Deborah Meier, describes the deeper
history of some of these ideas from her previous work in New York City
with the Central Park East schools, Lillian Weber, the Coalition of Essential
Schools, and others. Meier also argues that the purpose of public education must be to provide students with the skills of democracy: the ability to
deliberate, to listen to others' opinions, to search for new answers, to defend one's position with evidence, and to imagine a different future. Meier
reminds us that "schooling for ruling" was once reserved for the dominant
class in society, and now our hope must be for all students to learn to be
effective and powerful citizens in a democracy. The Mission Hill School
thus decided to create a more democratic, tracking-and-ranking-free

curriculum, one that treats all students as decisionmakers, even as students are widely diverse. All, not just some, students are smart. The school approaches all students with this in mind, encouraging them to reach for the stars and to create their best and most ambitious work, even as this work may be expressed in different ways.

In Chapter 3, Katherine Clunis D'Andrea, a Mission Hill School early childhood teacher of 16 years, describes her thinking as she approaches each of the thematic units she plans. In this chapter she focuses particularly on one thematic unit during the whole-school theme called "The World of Work." In her classroom, D'Andrea decided to follow her students' desire to learn about bread making and created a bakery within her own classroom. In this chapter, D'Andrea clearly struggles with the balance of planning for the 12-week unit well ahead of time while also listening and responding to the student's expressions of their immediate interests and curiosities. In the end, D'Andrea describes an inspiring curriculum that includes visiting with and learning from local bakers, choosing and baking delectable loaves and cupcakes, and challenging students to keep up with a large amount of math and literacy—all while students are being genuinely complimented and appreciated for their delicious efforts.

In Chapter 4, Geralyn Bywater McLaughlin, a teacher for more than 25 years at Mission Hill School and another school in the Boston area, describes how she thinks about creating curriculum for her early childhood students. She focuses within each theme on social and emotional development and the critical importance of providing time and opportunities for playing with various materials, people, and problems or challenges. Drawing on the theme "Garden Friends" within the schoolwide theme of "Natural Science," she argues and demonstrates that imagination, pretending, and play need to be front and center.

In Chapter 5, Jenerra Williams, a teacher for 12 years at Mission Hill School, describes how she thinks about designing curricula and focuses on her unit within the whole-school theme "The Struggle for Justice: U.S. History Through the Eyes of African Americans." Focusing on the civil rights movement, Williams uses photographs, songs, and poetry to help her 7- to 9-year-olds learn about and discuss the words *equality, courage,* and *justice* and to create art and expressions of moral reasoning on their own. Williams focuses on these essential understandings: (1) There is power in numbers and solidarity; (2) it takes courage to achieve justice and create change; and (3) art can tell the story of people's lives and experiences. Williams continually poses challenging questions to her students, such as "How can hearing or knowing someone's story change your viewpoint?" and "What rights do you fight for?"

In Chapter 6, Matthew Knoester, a teacher for 8 years at the Mission Hill School and other schools in Boston and in Minnesota, and someone who completed an in-depth study about the Mission Hill School involving interviews with 63 people intimately connected with the school and a survey of the graduates of the school, describes how he thinks about planning thematic curricula. He focuses on a particular thematic unit— "Astronomy"—within the schoolwide theme of "Physical Science" and describes how students studied the solar system and created model solar systems based on various historical perspectives. He also discusses the difficulty of balancing thematic teaching with pressure from standardized tests, especially in the area of math. Mission Hill teachers set aside an hour a day for math instruction, separate from the thematic unit, which has created new challenges.

In Chapter 7, one of the founding teachers, Jeanne Rachko, the whole-school art specialist, describes how she has approached teaching art, using the school's art room as a studio for students K–8. She begins by describing her unique use of the art room as both a whole-class teaching space and a place where just a few students can drop in at a time as they work on both long- and short-term projects. She then focuses on how she deliberated on and taught one particular whole-school theme, ancient China, and taught herself and then nearly every student in the school how to create art influenced by Chinese traditions, including creating chops (seals), watercolor paintings, Chinese characters, and Chinese opera masks. Rachko carefully balances the introduction of new traditions to students while also encouraging students to create art that uniquely expresses their own style and preferences. She describes how she supports the teaching of art in different teachers' classrooms and supports the aesthetic look of student projects and artistic displays throughout the school.

In Chapter 8, Heidi Lyne, one of the founding teachers at Mission Hill School, a teacher for more than 25 years, and currently a principal of another school in Boston, reflects on her teaching at Mission Hill. Lyne taught both 7- to 9-year-olds and 11- to 13-year-olds. In this chapter, she focuses on how to authentically assess student work at various age levels, with a particular focus on the Mission Hill graduation requirements. She describes her changing thinking on assessment over the years and the history of thinking on this topic at Mission Hill School and argues that the most useful and realistic form of assessment is performance based, centered on a portfolio of student work along with on-demand components.

In Chapter 9, the current principal of Mission Hill School, Ayla Gavins, reflects on the need to continually support professional development opportunities for teachers at the school. She describes examples of the professional development conducted by or for teachers, including sessions that focused on producing whole-school thematic units, and discusses how protocols, such as the descriptive review processes developed by Patricia Carini and others at the former Prospect Center in Vermont, allow teachers to powerfully interrogate assumptions they might have about individual children and to use community knowledge to solve difficult problems and generate solutions for many challenges facing teachers. Gavins focuses special attention on the suddenly and purposely enlarged inclusion of students who qualify for special education services in recent years and the rethinking it required about differentiation and inclusion. She describes how teachers continued to believe that whole-school thematic curricula was the most inclusive way to approach curricula and that long-range projects allowed students with many learning variations to gain access to subject material while avoiding the rigid tracking and separation that too often accompanies curriculum that is too focused on the assumption that large groups of students can have just one level of ability and set of skills.

In Chapter 10, Emily Gasoi, one of the founding teachers at Mission Hill School, and currently a new teacher mentor and educator in Washington, DC, examines the role that whole-school themes might play in the larger educational reform arena by cultivating a culture of continual school improvement. Drawing on her own experience with teaching thematic units and on interviews with teachers, Gasoi discusses how whole-school thematic units can affect the entire school community, providing powerful and enduring student learning; inviting family participation; and fostering a high degree of collegial communication, responsibility, and trust. While Gasoi does not assert that whole-school themes are a panacea for school improvement, her experience and research illuminate how whole-school, thematic teaching can support a school's capacity to engage in continual improvement while also providing students with habits of work and mind necessary for active democratic citizenship.

Finally, in Chapter 11, the Conclusion, the editors of the volume provide an overview and summary of the preceding chapters and underline the central arguments of the book: that the use of whole-school themes from kindergarten through 8th grade serves to strengthen community while also respecting the individuality of students of all ages and at all stages, with their different talents and abilities. In the process, staff, as well as students, are provided with peer support and offered expertise. Differentiating instruction to meet the needs of all learners is not an easy task, but whole-school thematic units constitute an approach that can build on the interests and strengths of all students. Further, we argue that performance-based assessments are the best use of time for teachers in supporting the work and development of students. Performances and student work that encourage artistry and attention to aesthetic appearance also offer students opportunities for the public recognition they need to create a positive student identity and to see themselves as serious learners who will challenge themselves to complete the best work possible.

The importance of play is also a key theme of the book. As is discussed in many chapters, children, as well as adults, need time and opportunities to play with new ideas, to be in a safe and comfortable setting where pressure to perform lets up and students are free to imagine how the world might be different if, for example, they poured water on this object or dressed up in that outfit or pretended to be a powerful deity in ancient Greece.

Chapter 11's authors note that it is impossible to describe all of the many aspects of the curricula that are named in this book and that visiting the school would provide a much richer perspective. However, another resource is available—a powerful film series that was created by Amy and Tom Valens and Sam Chaltain. In the Afterword, Tom and Amy Valens describe how they made the film series *A Year at Mission Hill*, and the film *Good Morning Mission Hill*, spending many hours in the school over the course of an entire school year and editing the film to focus on particular aspects of the school that they thought were unique and extraordinary. They reflect on the reception of the film and what they believe people should take away from both their film series and from this book.

The appedixes of the book include a table detailing the 4-year rotation of schoolwide themes; a list of the 5 habits of mind, the development of which is an educational goal across the curriculum; the mission statement of the school; and sample weekly newsletter.

We are excited to offer this work in the Practitioner Inquiry Series with Teachers College Press, as the editors of that series, Marilyn Cochran-Smith and Susan Lytle, and the contributors to this series, have highlighted the importance of teachers and educational practitioners critically reflecting on their work and sharing it with others (Cochran-Smith & Lytle, 1993, 2009). Critical practitioners, despite their intensive work loads, must continue to make public their views on education and refuse to be drowned out by voices and educational decisionmakers that spend little time in classrooms. We hope this book can provoke new ideas about what is possible in schools today, even as teachers and students seem to be facing ever greater restrictions regarding legitimate subject areas and the pace at which students and teachers must comply with standards.

REFERENCES

Cochran-Smith, M. & Lytle, S. L. (1993). *Inside/outside: Teacher research and knowledge*. New York, NY: Teachers College Press.

Cochran-Smith, M. & Lytle, S. L. (2009). *Inquiry as stance: Practitioner research for the next generation*. New York, NY: Teachers College Press.

Tomlinson, C. A., & McTighe, J. (2006). *Integrating differentiated instruction and understanding by design*. Alexandria, VA: Association for Supervision and Curriculum Development.

CHAPTER 2

Reflections on Mission Hill School's Early Years . . . and Before

Deborah Meier

This chapter consists of excerpts from publications of Deborah Meier, the founding principal of the Mission Hill School. The excerpts outline the thinking behind organizing the curriculum of the Mission Hill School into whole-school thematic units.

The following excerpt is from *Keeping School*, a collection of newsletters to families from school leaders (Meier, Sizer, & Sizer, 2004, pp. 34–36).

WHAT NOT TO TEACH?

We began the Mission Hill School with a basic principle: less is more. Better to cover well a few things than to cover everything poorly. But it's hard to resist. First one thing comes along, then another. They each seem so tempting. Occasionally we are saved by a budget crisis or by the ending of a grant. But we need also to be tougher on ourselves and to remember our mission to stay small and simple and to not try to be all things to all kids and families. This letter was the beginning of some tough reconsiderations about what we were trying to do. We'll never resolve this tension between all the stuff we think is important and teaching what's important well. We're likely to go back and forth. (We're fortunate that kids have another sixty years or so to "cover" the rest after they leave us.)

Every week during my time as principal at Mission Hill School we put together a school newsletter for parents and community members. The first page of the newsletter usually contained a letter from the principal. Here is a column I wrote in the school newsletter within the first few years of the school's opening:

Dear Families, Students, Staff, and Friends,

We are always getting great ideas. That's in the nature of being human. Lots of them are so good they are hard to resist. But there's a price to pay.

National panels of education experts meet and decide that this or that subject is vitally important and schools ought to teach it. The problem, of course, is finding time to add every new thing to the already stuffed curriculum. The experts solve this problem partly by pushing things to earlier and earlier grades and ages.

As Americans become more aware of other nations' concerns, schools are told to study them. As scientists' knowledge of the universe grows more complex, we're told to start teaching science earlier to get it all in. Everyone thinks his specialty is the most important: how can you call yourself well educated without having studied Asian history, or economics, or number theory, or nineteenth-century literature, or Italian art—not to mention without having studied how to have a balanced diet and do a PowerPoint presentation?

Within each of the major subjects the number of topics that seem "critical" grows and grows. One education research lab did a study of new state curriculum frameworks and concluded that we would have to add nine more years of schooling just to cover all the required topics. The framework writers are only too happy to tell teachers what to add; they never say what to subtract.

At Mission Hill, we try to resist. Our four-year curriculum cycle and our five habits of mind help us focus on what's important within each subject area. But we, too, add, and we don't often subtract. We added string instrument lessons in year two, then hired an art teacher, then added band instruments, then chorus. We've tried various approaches to teaching theater and drama (Urban Improv and now Shakespeare & Company). We added Spanish this year.

But at what price? I'm referring not just to the money these additions cost but the time. When kids are studying any of the above, what are they not studying?

It's not easy to decide what not to teach. It feels awkward, uncomfortable, heartless. Nevertheless, it's time for some hard thinking on this issue. The change in schedule for next year gives us a good opportunity to revisit our priorities. Lots of private schools solve the time problem partly by placing "extras" before and after school, as options, or electives. This forces families to make choices, and leaves the bulk of the already short school day free for the essentials.

The trouble is that one person's extra is another's essential. It won't be easy, but thinking these things out and speaking about them will get us closer to where we want to go.

The following first appeared in Chapter 10 of *In Schools We Trust* (Meier, 2002, pp. 176–180).

For me the most important answer to the question "Why save public education?" is this: It is in schools that we learn the art of living together as citizens, and it is in public schools that we are obliged to defend the idea of a public, not only a private, interest.

Debates, for instance, over what constitutes appropriate or inappropriate play yard behavior and how best to punish wrongdoers are mirrors of our larger struggles over what being a good citizen is and over what justice should look like. Schools are where we learn about the possible meanings of patriotism—what it means to own one's community and have a stake in its reputation. How much more tenuous such relationships are when schools become huge, their decision-making apparatus invisible or far distant, and when citizens no longer feel connected to their children's schools. In only slightly over half a century we've gone from having two hundred thousand school boards to fewer than twenty thousand—serving at least twice as many youngsters.

It is within schools that we can learn how to live with such uneasy balances, even cherish them—even as we naturally are often averse to doing so! The odds must be stacked against any too easy escape from the annoyances of our fellow citizens. It's within our schools, and in the governance of them, that we need to learn how to resist institutional and peer pressures, as well as respect the institutions we live with and the peers who are our fellow citizens. It's in such institutions that we need to learn to handle authority in all its many forms—both legitimate and illegitimate—and how to take authority on—effectively. It's within such schools that we need to learn to resist what we see as improper encroachments on our rights, and to organize and expand what we believe to be our entitlements. All the habits of mind and work that go into democratic institutional life must be practiced in our schools until they truly become habits—so deeply a part of us that in times of stress we fall back on them rather than abandon them in search of a great leader or father figure, or retreat into the private isolation of our private interests, the unfettered marketplace where one need not worry about the repercussions of one's individual decisions.

Like the learning of all important things, the learning of these democratic habits of mind happens only when children are in the real company of adults they trust and when adults have sufficient powers—and the leisure—to be good company. On the largest political scale, this is why I worry so much about—and work so hard to change—the way children are growing up without adult company, a community of elders. In some ways we accept our children's adulthood long before we once did, and in other ways we continue to treat them as children for far longer. We fear for them as we never did before, thus protecting them from independent play before and after school, and restricting even the kind of play they once engaged in at lunch and recess. Thus, while school occupies only a fifth of kids' waking hours, the institutions we've invented for the rest of the day are remarkably similar—only for many kids far shabbier and less well funded. And in the time left over, the mass media provide a highly compelling world for the young, who spend considerably more time watching the screen than talking to any adults. And, of course, they sneak off together in packs to browse around their favorite meeting places, shopping malls, where they are, once again, consumers amid strangers whom surely they would be wise not to trust.

The consequences of our interpersonal estrangement are not obvious, even as there is a growing literature on the topic, and I quite frankly am only beginning my exploration. I don't know what all this means in terms of personality development, neurosis, stress, illness, intimacy, and long-term relationship building. There may even be some positives that we will learn to celebrate and nourish. But I do think I begin to see dangerous signs of what such estrangement does to the creation of potentially viable democratic communities.

Democracy assumes the prior existence of communities of people with shared loyalties, confidences, and understandings. It doesn't create them—they are far older and more persistent than modern (or even ancient) democracies. We have always taken such communities for granted. They were an inevitable byproduct of being human beings. What got me nervous was the erosion of such naturally forming communities—or at least their formation in ways quite different than we as humans have ever known before. It's not always easy to know when something new is merely a new wrinkle or a dangerous breakdown of civilization. Crisis talk always worries me, so I say this with trepidation.

. . . But modern democratic and pluralistic societies require trust even when their members are, in fact, very different from each other. We need to be able to count on each other most of the time to act "as if" we are trustworthy, even as we also know that we will often enough have our trust betrayed. We are shocked (naively?) by politicians' machinations to undermine the democratic process. But much as we must learn from such betrayals, we need to learn to cope with them in ways that neither abandon the idea of democracy nor undermine our sense of community. We still need to assume that it is not beyond reason to view the world as more or less trustworthy—that things can make some sense, including both those natural phenomena that so often seem puzzling and the many equally perplexing human relationships. I fall back on Winston Churchill's pithy reminder that democracy may well be "the worst form of government except for all the other forms which have been tried from time to time."

We need to know the nature of the connections between ourselves and the planet, to test out our powers over the material world, to recognize our limitations; we need to know when to sit back and get pleasure from the world we didn't make—as we gradually understand better and acknowledge its ultimate unknowability. So too with our connections to our fellow beings, who are equally unknowable in any ultimate sense. We cannot actually "be" others; we can only stretch our well-informed imaginations. This is what many scientists remind me is at the heart of a good science education: allowing kids time to play with the world, lie back in awe to take in the sky, dig holes to China, watch the dominoes topple over and over and over again.

Modern life requires an appreciation for the complexity and interconnectedness of people and other living things, if we have any hope of maintaining both the planet and our democratic institutions. And since those are my hopes, I'm counting a lot on our ability to build a system of schooling that helps reforge such connections.

The following can be found in *Keeping School* (Meier, Sizer, & Sizer, 2004, pp. 22–24).

THE WAY WE TEACH

Despite numerous attempts, we haven't succeeded in answering the question that motivated this column: is Mission Hill tough enough? Some assume we teach the way we do because it's easier. It's not. Some think we're not rigorous enough in our demands. Since rigor means harsh and unbending, we plead guilty—but not to being too soft. We think our five habits of mind are tough to master and that few kids leaving our school (and few of us adults) have mastered them so thoroughly that we always use them in times of stress. But our nine-year curriculum is meant to get kids in certain habits of mind that will be hard to break, even when easier paths offer themselves. We learn good habits best when the rewards that come from learning are foremost in our minds. So we keep hammering away at it.

Here is a column I wrote in the *Mission Hill School News:*

Dear Families, Students, Staff, and Friends,

Do you wonder how we plan curriculum—in math, science, history, or literature? Here's a rough description of the process. We start off with an idea, an experience, a time and place, or a problem. We brainstorm among ourselves about where it might take both us and the kids, and then we read up on the subject, find lots of possible materials, and decide how to launch it. Sometimes we brainstorm a way to cap off our study at the end.

As we teach, we look for connections to our children's own questions and interests, and we notice which ideas and activities seem most engaging to the group. No two classes, or kids, are the same. Those five habits of mind are our constant guide. We try always to be sure that each topic of study lends itself to the development of those habits and we keep pushing everyone to use them. We also try to be sure that as we study a particular topic or phenomenon kids have lots of opportunities to read about it, model it, talk and write about it, and, if possible, measure it. In short, we try to connect whatever they are studying to practical skills, to the basic disciplines of academia, and to their own special interests and talents—their strengths. Equally important, we want them to fall in love with at least some aspect of what we are engaged in. And all the time we provoke, question, and extend—and offer a lot of feedback.

We have an eight-year curriculum plan designed to ensure a balance between important contemporary social issues, the ancient history of various cultures, and physical and biological science. The whole school follows this plan so that we can provide staff and students with a lot more depth and breadth. Each larger theme comes up twice over the nine-year span, which adds more depth and breadth to our studies.

Over the next few weeks, I'll try to explain why we plan curriculum this way. There is research evidence that our method helps develop the kind of intellectual competence, curiosity, and skill that pays off in high school, college, the workplace, and everyday life. We know there are other ways, but we believe this is the most efficient.

Of course, sometimes we also teach traditional lessons within these broad thematic studies, with precise objectives that all kids focus on, such as memorizing key words or geography terms. And we study topics specific to reading, writing, and math at times set aside for these narrower subjects. Even then, we aim for a balance between a thematic approach and specific directed teaching.

We're going to organize study groups to read and talk about this way of teaching and learning so that those who'd like to can become more expert. At the heart of our philosophy is the importance of asking good questions—so don't be afraid to ask them.

The following first appeared in *In Schools We Trust* (Meier, 2002, pp. 20–23).

Despite vast differences, there are some commonalities in terms of the relationships between teachers and learners in the schools that work to build the intellectual skills of all kids.

First: schools that work are safe. We know that infants require safety to thrive, but so do school-age kids. The more time that must be devoted to protecting oneself from bodily or mental harm—from peers or authorities—the less energy there is left to devote to other tasks. Creating safety for kids with a diversity of histories and goals means more than just making them physically safe—it includes helping them to feel safe from ridicule and embarrassment.

Second: schools that work do their best to reproduce the ratios that make for successful learning—that is, the number of experts per novice. That means not only the ratio of teachers to students but also the range of expertise available to kids—other adults, older students, and students with different skills and abilities, not to mention varied learning tools (computers, books, real-life learning experiences). The ways are varied: small classes, multiple-age classes, older students working with younger ones, adult volunteers, activities that cut across age and skill levels. Successful schools are always looking for those magical relationships—the ones that break down the barriers.

Third: schools that work make it possible for those precious experts—even if they are only slightly more expert—to show their stuff, to display and demonstrate both their passion and their skill in highly personal ways (not just to talk about what they're good at but actually to do their stuff alongside of novices). Sharing expertise—copying—is viewed not as cheating but as a useful way of learning. We learn best alongside people we rather like, who can't resist showing us this or that amazing pattern, even if it isn't part of their official duty. Coming across hundreds of snails in our schoolyard for the first time launched an unexpected but irresistible study of snail life. How wonderful it was for our children to learn that there are famous scientists who study snails (and make a living at it) all their lives.

Fourth: schools that work offer a range of ways for learners to find their way around any new domain of knowledge, and more than one way to become good at science or history. Successful schools take it for granted that mistakes have a logic to them that needs to be uncovered, not just corrected. Placing objects such as a nail or a heavy box or a sliver of wood in a body of water and exploring what happens, probing tactfully—"what would happen if you added this?"—can lead to fascinating discoveries, but this approach takes expertise, plus an open scientific mind-set, if it is to lead to "aha's" for most of us. Even then not all of us will come to the aha's through one particular experiment alone. There need to be other openings for discussing the differences between density, mass, and weight—which initially may seem identical. When a thirteen-year-old said to me over lunch the other day, "Do you know, if I tried to count to a billion it would take me a lifetime?" how delighted she was that after all these years of being an adult I was for a moment skeptically astonished. But she's right—as we figured out together. Whether we take in new ideas as babies by exploring the nature of the objects in our environment with hands and mouth, or later on by measuring objects on a scale, over and over again, or by calculating how many seconds it would take to get to a billion, we are doing the same thing: making ideas ours. Once they are ours, they don't seem counterintuitive anymore—or, equally important, they don't seem like nonsense. We now have a basis for making sense of not just this one thing but many more.

Fifth: such schools offer plenty of time for ideas to grow, and they don't set rigid timetables. For some kids the aha's are almost immediate; others require seemingly endless repetitions—just in case next time it will come out differently. Besides, such qualities of patience are to be cherished and are, after all, part of the scientific tradition. Although making a flat map out of a round globe does what no book-based explanation of map distortion can achieve—try it!—it's a waste of precious time if we think about it as an exercise in coverage rather than in understanding.

Sixth: schools built around this model of learning do their best to make schooling engaging and fun. Engagement and pleasure help focus the mind, keep one persevering, and encourage repeated practice. Pain may occasionally teach us a lesson, but not as a regular routine, and the lesson it most often teaches is avoidance. This means filling up the classroom with stuff of interest that couldn't help but fascinate and leads to questions, ideas, experiments. It means including both ordinary materials—sand, dirt, and water—in new contexts, more exotic ones—centipedes and monarch butterflies—that amaze, or unusual ideas that can't actually be seen or touched but fascinate— like the distance to the moon. And adding to these collections of things and ideas are all those books—including beautiful ones—that might illuminate students' questions. It helps (for many reasons) for kids to see themselves, their communities, and their stories reflected in what is studied—but often in new and unexpected contexts. Ulysses' boasts are familiar, after all, as he endangers himself and his men just to get in the last word to the Cyclops. Good schools have ways to latch on to kids' idiosyncratic passions as well—their love of cars or wrestlers even—in the formal instructional day as well as after school, on Saturdays, and during the summer.

Seventh: such schools know that what one is learning needs to have lots of possible hooks to other things and thus lends itself to being practiced in the normal course of living. Suddenly, as soon as you're studying a new subject, it seems that the whole world is talking about what you've just learned! Studying about American politics when it's election year or the Supreme Court when there's a major debate over who is to be selected to sit on the high court makes getting the most out of such subjects far easier. Many high school teaching colleagues and I missed a great opportunity in the early nineties when we ignored the breakup of the Soviet empire and just kept on with our self-prescribed course of study. We did better when the world became so much more frightening for us all on September 11, 2001. We took the time to explore the unsettling immediacies of the moment in depth and thoughtfulness with our older students. (For many teachers of tenth graders these days, changing the course outline in light of the changed course of history is literally to risk children's educational futures—and their own—in light of state exams.) But studying about ancient Greece last year for all the kids from kindergarten through eighth grade didn't seem irrelevant either. The students ran across so much stuff with Greek motifs in the daily press, magazines, buildings, stories, and everyday language. I have seen elementary school students and high school kids take to ancient Egypt with an even greater zeal. It turns out to be a favorite regardless of age, second only to dinosaurs—so there must be hoods we don't always recognize.

The next section is from "Experiments in Trust: The Mission Hill School and Others," Chapter 2 of *In Schools We Trust* (Meier, 2002, pp. 26–40).

The small schools I know best are public schools, intentionally invented after bigness was the norm—starting in the late sixties and early seventies in cities and suburbs all across the nation. They were created from scratch in part because smallness was appealing, but mostly because they represented a different vision of what it meant to educate all children well, and what it would take to do so within the public sector. And at the center were a series of ideas about the educative importance of respect for the human penchant for learning and about the role of adults—at home and at school—in preserving and extending this natural talent.

Of course, there have always been kids who make it despite what appear to be adverse environments: big impersonal schools or schools that perhaps purposely insist that children renounce their home culture. There are kids who even seem to benefit from keeping school and family in separate airtight compartments. But for the vast majority of learners, it helps when their learning works in concert with their home and community, not in conflict with them, and expands upon the learners' known universe, rather than denying or trying to forget a part of it. And for this to happen, adults in schools need to truly know the children they serve over many years, something almost impossible in traditional huge schools.

My experience with putting these ideas into practice beyond my own classroom began with efforts to create small adult communities within big anonymous city schools. Creating interesting places for teachers to learn was where my reform agenda began. An extraordinary woman named Lillian Weber was teaching early childhood education at City College when I arrived in New York City in the fall of 1966. She pointed to the loneliness of the teaching profession as a serious roadblock to good work with children. It isn't enough, she insisted, that we love our own twenty-five to thirty children, or even that we respect their families, although those were necessary starting points. Weber argued that both children and adults needed to be part of a community of learning. Her wedge into the big schools was called the "open corridor." She found principals willing to put three, four, or five interested teachers, often of different grade levels, next to each other along one corridor—while ostensibly supervising her student teachers. She created communities of adults and kids where their respective work was public and visible to families, colleagues, and peers. She built minischools in these corridors. They were fragile, rarely lasting more than a few years, but they whetted our appetite for more.

Lillian made us pay attention to all the learning that was taking place quite efficiently in unexpected places, the instructive interactions that we didn't count as instructional time. We were reminded of the extensive evidence of the centrality of play in human learning—and the terrible cost, both emotional and intellectual, when playfulness is aborted early and too often. She made us more aware of what kids already knew before they arrived at school and what they continued to learn before and after school from their families and communities. We began to think in new ways about our own learning histories, our enthusiasms and confusions, and how we could learn from other adults in ways that could make the school a productive complement to children's learning.

Central Park East (CPE) grew out of Lillian Weber's work; this school was simply an "open corridor" that was more permanent, less dependent on the annual vagaries of a principal. District 4 in East Harlem, considered at the time the least successful district in New York City, made me a proposal: would I like to start "my own public school"? It was too appealing to turn down—especially given the gathering storm clouds of centralization, back to basics, and more and more testing that was driving the system in the early seventies. I gathered friends from Lillian's workshop center at City College. We asked only for rooms near each other, enough autonomy to work out another way of teaching kids that might get better results, and a system whereby parents would be given a choice about joining or not joining our community.

In less than five years there were three elementary CPEs in East Harlem, and shortly afterward we organized a CPE secondary school (CPESS), and over the next few decades dozens and dozens more on the same model just in New York City. For a time, our bottom-up reform ideas were even faddishly popular, as the various standardized solutions bottomed out. It became commonplace to hear college education majors talk about starting their own little public school, as though this were one of the long-standing career options available in life. (And, we would argue, had the policy arm of the educational establishment listened to us and devoted anywhere near the same energy, focus, and resources as they periodically devote to standardization, the total number of such little schools would have increased exponentially.)

What these schools set out to do, although they weren't always aware of it, was to tackle the problem described in Chapter 1: to change the nature of the company kids and teachers keep, to build a trusting and trustworthy community, and thus to help children learn in more efficient and natural ways. In the year 2000 the nearly forty small New York public high schools that came out of this period of work put together sufficiently compelling data to convince even a group of reputable and established test experts gathered together by a hostile commissioner of education that they were onto something important. The schools' graduation and subsequent college attendance rates, for kids that met everyone's definition of "at risk," were hard to explain in conventional terms. Of Central Park East high school students, for instance, 90 percent graduated and 90 percent of those went on to college, in a city where the average dropout rate was 50 percent. The group of test experts convened by the commissioner to put an end to these maverick schools came out in tentative support of them instead. What they were witnesses to, I claim, is the power of such schools to build relationships that educate, in contrast to institutions that can't because they are organized to ignore, if not exclude, such relationships.

In 1994 I retired from teaching in the New York public school system to join Ted Sizer at the newly funded Annenberg Institute for School Reform in order to support efforts to make such forms of schooling more systematically feasible. But one day in the spring of 1996 I found myself on a long drive to Boston—with a broken radio. So I had time to dream, and I found myself dreaming of starting another elementary school. By the time I got to Boston, I was bursting with the idea. Boston, I knew, had just begun a little systemic approach to reinventing schools, sponsoring small pilot schools with much of the autonomy of charter schools but embedded firmly within the city's public system. It was the brainchild of the local Boston teachers' union, and it was hard to resist. At sixty-five, I found the idea of taking on a new little city appealing, and Boston wasn't much farther from my new home base in upstate New York than New

York City had been. I gathered some Boston and Cambridge friends, we wrote a proposal, and we were accepted—to start a pilot school in the fall of 1997 in an old vacated church school in the Roxbury section of Boston. The building would be shared with a new pilot high school. Between us we'd have about 350 students, a floor each to ourselves and some shared spaces. I was back to where I began, with a few differences, principally a much more conscious awareness of the issues of accountability and trust. When I started at CPE, I had mostly been focused on simply creating a safe haven for me and some friends to do what we thought right. The student population was somewhat different too—although overwhelmingly a population of color, there were fewer Latinos, more middle-class students, and more whites—20 to 25 percent.

The Mission Hill School, like many of the other small schools I know, was deliberately designed to make it hard for the adult culture and the youth culture to hang apart for long. We even tried to make it easy for the high school and elementary school to exchange people and ideas. We shared a secretary the first year, and a social worker, a nurse, and, above all, ideas and camaraderie. Even in terms of physical space, we thought about how to make the generations overlap. At Mission Hill Elementary, the main office—located right in the heart of our main floor—serves as the workspace for the full-time administration (me, Brian Straughter, and the school manager, Marla Gaines), as well as a portal for parents coming and going, for teachers picking up mail and using the copier, for most phone calls, not to mention being the place "bad" kids cool off, good kids retreat to, and everyone leaves messages—who's out that day, who has gone to do an errand, and so forth. The grown-up behind-the-scenes life of the school is made visible and touchable. Kids come in and out to use the copier, the phones, and just to say hello and see what's up. We don't have to lecture them about this place belonging to all of us—it does.

We got this idea of shared space in part from Urban Academy, a small high school in New York City, where the staff have desks surrounded by their own bookcases and file drawers, a niche that expresses their unique interests, all in one huge room. The kids come in and out to see teachers and discuss their work. It's like the floor of the stock exchange. Everything that's going on is right there. Usually hushed and quiet and busy and important. The Mission Hill main office is a miniversion of that.

The hallways and lobbies of such schools work best if we think of them as the marketplaces in small communities—where gossip is exchanged, work displayed, birthdays taken note of; where clusters of kids and adults gather to talk, read, and exchange ideas. It's Lillian Weber's "open corridor" forty years later. Mission Hill's hallways are a marketplace of goods and ideas that cross ages—from the youngest to the oldest. We were lucky because the seventy-five-year-old building was designed with fourteen-foot-wide corridors.

We organized our very small school into two even smaller identical clusters, each occupying half the floor. Half the five-year-olds start with Alicia Carroll, with whom they spend two years; then they move across the hall to Emily Gasoi (and now Jenerra Williams) for two years, then on to Alphonse Litz, and finally to Ayla Gavins and Heidi Lyne and the middle school team. Four or five teachers thus get to know eighty kids so well that being accountable for them happens naturally, without complex articulation plans or reporting schemes. In schools in which children work with new teachers every year, each teacher would effectively have to get to know twice as many students. In addition, the Mission Hill teachers know exactly where the kids they have had for two years are headed next— right across the hall. At the other end, Kathy Clunis, Geralyn McLaughlin, James McGovern (and now Matthew Knoester), Roberta Logan, and Emily Chang constitute a second minicommunity. The seventh and eighth graders naturally grow into being the leaders of the school—taking on new jobs as they seem appealing and useful. A group of kids begged (Tom Sawyer fashion) to organize the end-of-the-day bus dismissal—which involves having to use cell phones. Others took on our Friday morning assembly, where students share work in progress—leading the little kids in singing songs the older students might shun if they were only part of the audience.

We aim to create an intense adult community of learners that will entice kids to want to belong too. To increase the odds, we are constantly on the lookout for ways kids can join adult activities wherever we can find a space or interest. When we're all studying about ancient Egypt, the hall turns into the Nile River with important landmarks along the way, and amateur Egyptologists join us. Joyce Stevens, our curriculum consultant, is often ensconced in the hall, à la Lillian Weber, with odd and interesting objects and an inquiring mind.

It grows. Youngsters at Mission Hill borrow the computers in the class next door or the office when their own are being used. They stop to chat with grown-ups, take books from the library, read what is on the walls— kid stuff or grown-up stuff—take pride in knowing everyone and being known. Because all of us, from five-year-olds to seventy-year-olds, study the same Big Themes at the same time, the corridor takes on a unifying role. The big schoolwide themes are both enticing and constraining. We ask ourselves often, is the trade-off going to be worth the loss of the individual teachers' autonomy to decide what to concentrate on? Are schoolwide themes developmentally sensible? Just as we ask ourselves whether the easy access kids have to the copier, the phone, and our semiprivate messages might sometimes backfire. Some of these practices, after all, were dictated more by lack of space than by design. But as time passes, we see these by-products as plusses (although with occasional minuses!). As you walk down the halls of our school or schools like ours, or in and out of these classrooms, you are struck by how much conversation is taking place and how often it crosses age boundaries. Kids begin to use grown-up phrases, to try out the intellectual jargon of their teachers—at least some of the time. Of course, one reciprocal effect is that we adults also find ourselves slipping into the jargon of our youngsters.

It mattered that as a Boston pilot school we were allowed to pick our staff, develop alternate school-based policies where our working rules conflicted with the teachers' union contract, use our equal per capita funds more flexibly, and in general more or less set our own course, within the confines of Massachusetts state education law. We receive no more money per student than any other Boston public school, but we made spending choices that allowed us to reduce class sizes by effectively hiring more teachers. Doing so meant that from the start we reduced class sizes to twenty students (compared with a citywide average of over twenty-five) and added a full-time paid adult-in-training to each class. Some of these adults came from regular teacher education institutions, and some came just to explore the possibility of becoming teachers. We also discovered that class sizes and pupil-teacher ratios are like closet space—critical, and there's never enough. We didn't have to scramble for a building, although of course we had to hustle to see that it was properly remodeled, renovated, and kept up. That first fall we opened without furniture.

Much of the day kids are working independently or in small groups, which probably is one reason visitors think we have few serious discipline problems or especially needy or learning-disabled youngsters. Both are harder to detect, although in fact our student population is pretty representative of Boston's overall demographics. (Our students are chosen through Boston's universal citywide lottery system based, in part, on parental choice, and over which we have no control.)

Given the importance of adult talk time, we put aside monies that in another school might have gone into hiring another staff position in order that each full-time core faculty member was paid to "think like a principal"—for the time and extra work involved in intimately being a part of and responsible for the conduct of the whole school—from designing curriculum to evaluating colleagues. The freedom to allocate our funds in our own way made it easier to ensure that we'd put in the extra time that any good school needs from its members. Researchers have noted that American schools expect teachers to spend more time instructionally and less time preparing for their work than any system in the advanced world. We decided to do something about this. The Mission Hill staff agreed, regardless of stipend, to work together for five hours a week after the school day was over, as well as three weeks over the summer, one professional retreat day midyear, and the regular citywide professional days. It turned out to be not enough. But it meant we could move into ways of working that many of the teachers had never tried before, to create a community for adults and kids alike around common topics, to be largely self-governing—and thus accountable far faster than otherwise. If trust requires accountability, accountability requires time.

Of course, spending more on staff development and planning time—and smaller class sizes—meant spending less elsewhere: we hired no full-time specialists in foreign languages or physical education, and we had no self-contained special education services or supply clerks. Even music was reduced to part-timers. We bought fewer individual student and teacher desks, and we spent virtually zero on individual class textbooks.

The extra time together as teachers meant we could immediately tackle the question of the standards for graduating our eighth graders. As Heidi Lyne describes later in this book, we designed a system, modeled roughly on the one we used in New York City's small high schools. We started with many fewer older students, so that we could try out our graduation requirements first on a small scale. In June 2001, all twelve of our first graduates completed the arduous, pioneering adventure (some of them complained of being "guinea pigs") of preparing, presenting, defending, and in many cases re-presenting many times their six portfolios before their Graduation Committees. These six portfolios are aimed at demonstrating to a committee of five (composed of one external critic, a younger student, two faculty members, and a family member) that the student has lived up to the school's standards of work and habits of mind in history, literature, art, science, math—plus something we've called "beyond the classroom." In each area, graduating students need a body of work that demonstrates consistent habits of work and intellectual competence, as well as the ability to present and expand on such work in a public way. The record of this committee's findings and the student's work become part of the school's permanent archive. We also videotape a sample of sessions for our own and public purposes. We held our breath near the end. The first twelve, just barely making their deadlines in time to cross the stage at our first graduation, moved on to a high school of their choice.

We also undertook to develop varied ways to collect hard data. We interview—on an ongoing tape—every child as a reader twice a year. We collect and score writing samples. We conduct standardized math interviews. We hold exhibitions of children's work. We visit each other's classrooms. We invent questionnaires and surveys to tap into student engagement and family connectedness. We compare our hard data to the test data we also have and any other available standard indicators—attendance, transfers, tardiness, suspensions. We do this mostly to improve our work, and to see whether we have confounded the odds that predict that some kids won't reach high standards. We look at the data in every which way—separating them by class, race, gender, and how long kids have been with us. This wide range of evidence of student work is our way to demonstrate to children's families and the broader public our trustworthiness. Its value lies precisely in the fact that it is open to different interpretations and judgments.

The judgments we make are exercises in the use of the same five habits of mind we commend so highly to our students: (1) looking at the data from several different viewpoints, (2) questioning the validity and reliability of the evidence, (3) looking for patterns across subjects and time, (4) making hypotheses, wondering how else we might have done something, and how else it might have turned out. In the end the work must meet the test that "it matters." This fifth habit of mind is perhaps the one that's hardest for schools to get right, and the most important to the kids.

In a small school like Mission Hill, kids can pick and choose, as over the years they develop new relationships with the adults—in a school purposely designed for falling in love with new experiences and people, the odds of each student finding a life-changing adult outside of his or her family circle is extraordinarily great. When students are preparing to graduate, we select an adult who is not currently one of their teachers to act as adviser, to guide them through the portfolio process. We also picked up on a successful CPESS practice—community service. Invented as much to provide teachers with free time as anything, it turned out to have life-changing repercussions for entirely different reasons. Over the four years that students spent doing community service, almost all, according to interviews conducted in later years, had built at least one relationship with an adult that helped them get into college, find a job, build a network in a larger world. We fashioned something similar for all youngsters in grades six through eight at Mission Hill. In addition, our part-time school social worker, Delores Costello, uses her knowledge of kids and families to find all manner of experiences for each family and child—scholarships for one-of-a-kind sleepaways (e.g., Alvin Ailey camp), Saturday art programs, or museum offerings. We brought musicians into school so that kids could sit at their feet, listen, watch, and imagine being them (which led, in turn, to hiring a string teacher to teach violin and cello). As the graduates of Central Park East reported to us years later in trying to account for their unusual success, the school had not only acknowledged and nourished their own particular interests, but also sought ways to link them to other people who in the end were life-inspiring.

Boston's Isabella Stewart Gardner Museum, with its stuffy nineteenth-century unchanged European art exhibit, has become a familiar second home to many of our students, thanks to the imaginative adults who have organized its education program. Our kids go there now, greet the guards and curators with respectful familiarity, and make themselves at home in the best sense. Parents tell us that when they go to the neighboring Museum of Fine Arts kids casually guide them through the familiar Egyptian exhibit, the ancient Chinese rooms, and the Greek sections—comparing, contrasting, and pointing to particular beloved works of art they have become familiar with. Students tell stories, based on close observations over the years, about our neighborhood and Boston, stories connected to schoolwide themes about the history of Boston and its people. All of these cultural experiences are powerful because they are mediated by relationships with people the students have come to know and see as familiar.

A staff that looks and sounds like the kids and their families, in terms of race, style, and ethnicity, is another asset when trying to build trust. At Mission Hill the majority of classroom teachers and administrators, for example, are people of color. This is the fastest and most efficient way to assure kids that the experiences the school opens up for them are not always "white" or "black," but belong to them all. Having a staff that even partially mirrors the makeup of the students also increases the odds that the conversations among the adults partake of the languages the children are accustomed to at home and see as theirs. I realize how nice it is that talk in the high school lapses into Spanish so often. Using the students' own languages sends reassuring messages. It allows some things to go unsaid while sending a message of respect.

The work described in this book is made much more difficult by the Massachusetts Comprehensive Assessment System (MCAS), a grade-three-through-twelve testing program with high stakes attached. It was a testing system antithetical to everything Mission Hill represented in terms of both curriculum and pedagogy. The new and controversial regime required working out a stance that could be supported by staff and parents alike. Although many opposed the tests, some parents also feared for their children's futures in a society that would judge them by their test results. Such concerns had to be taken seriously. Faculty members also worried about making kids take a test that they had intentionally not taught to the way other colleagues in the city had—especially in history and science. Our school was clearly running against the grain of a testing system built on distrust, and it not only made us bristle but also conflicted with our methods and aims.

At worst, our practice lowers our cumulative school score (since students who do not take the test are given a zero score), and thus our ranking, and could perhaps (if the city or state chose) lead to threats against us. If we were a high school, of course, the risks for kids and families would be greater. Many families choose for their kids to take one or another of the other standardized tests periodically administered in Boston just to see how they stack up, and we regularly provide families and kids access to tests if they want to see what they're like. On the whole we were able to provide some evidence for our claim that kids would do as well in the long run even on tests. It remained hard for parents, kids, and teachers to operate against the grain, but doing so enabled us to avoid having to reorganize our curriculum or pedagogy to match the frequently changing state frameworks and tests. (In some states, penalty-free opt-outs for parents are now state-mandated.)

The ancient Greeks knew what they were about when they said that democratic governance was the province of the leisured classes. (The word for school and leisure are one and the same in Greek.) It takes time to be thoughtful. How can space for the exercise of judgment in governance be translated into school life? This is our number one problem. It will be yours too, we told the folks from Oakland. We wanted a leisurely lunch and recess time for the kids, but we wanted the same for the adults who worked in the building—time to go to the bathroom, to use the phone, to get hold of needed supplies, to talk to colleagues, or just to eat in the private and sublime silence. We managed it. But we still ache for more adult leisure time to work things out, and finding ways to staff the kid part of that midday break is full of trade-offs. Of course, we'll never know what the other side of all these trade-offs might have produced. So we try to forgive ourselves for our failures, even as we keep them in view.

Different schools will invent different ways to establish their unique culture—often diametrically opposite ways—as well as make their unique mistakes. That's a hopeful fact rather than a discouraging one. The kids calling us by our first names is an important symbol of our shared culture, for example. But I know that the kind of learning environment we have created here also exists in schools that insist on last names, even uniforms. What doesn't work are schools that think we can be made uniform, that the messy business of learning to deal with each other can be bypassed by rules imposed by people who don't know us in all our particularities.

In a school with so much easy access to each other, the odds are that it won't always be smooth going—maybe sometimes even less so than in big and more impersonal schools. The culture of a school that is organized the way Mission Hill is brings questions of trust—between parents and schools, among teachers, between children and teachers—to the fore in a way that is perhaps unique in American education. The power of trust makes these schools run and makes them educative. The potential downfalls that come with trust are what make them difficult—and exciting—places to work. As the following chapters explore, the way trust plays itself out, or not, is all in the details—and the details, almost without exception, are never finished.

I hope the chapters of this book help to flesh out the decisionmaking and curricular organization that led to what I believe was not a perfect, but very good, way to approach the challenges of teaching the habits of mind for democratic education. Enjoy!

REFERENCES

Meier, D. W. (2002). *In schools we trust: Creating communities of learning in an era of testing and standardization.* Boston, MA: Beacon Press.

Meier, D. W., Sizer, T. R., & Sizer, N. F. (2004). *Keeping school: Letters to families from principals of two small schools.* Boston, MA: Beacon Press.

CHAPTER 3

What's Baking?

Learning Together about Bread and Bakeries

Katherine Clunis D'Andrea

I expressed to my 5- to 7-year-old students my interest in learning about bakeries for our "World of Work" theme, wondering how they might respond. When several students expressed interest during our morning meeting one day I asked all the students, "What do you want to learn about bakeries?" They wrote in their journals and drew pictures. Alejandro wrote, "Do they have doughnuts?" Zayna wrote, "I want to know if they make all the food or they buy some of it?" Cyrus wrote, "I want to know if bakeries get the ingredients for the food that they make or they make the ingredients." Rafael wrote, "I want to learn how to make everything." Already, the different experiences that children had had with bakeries were starting to form our study.

Cooking has become an important part of the weekly routine in my classroom, and we engage in this activity even when we are not studying bakeries. Cooking helps children build science, literacy, math, and social skills. Each Monday we make something different. When I first started our "World of Work" unit I shared with the children that we would have to bake every day for the bakery. They were excited and ready. We baked on the Monday and then Tuesday morning came and I said that we would be baking again. Andrew yelled in approval, with joy, "We are baking again!" For the next 2 weeks we baked every day and the children developed a real taste of what working might be like.

DEVELOPING THEMATIC UNITS

For the past 16 years I have been a teacher at the Mission Hill School in Boston, Massachusetts. Since Mission Hill School is a project-based, staff-run, urban, multiage, pilot public school that teaches using school-wide themes, I have learned how essential teaching in themes is for students' learning. There is an importance to the interconnectedness of subjects that makes learning real for children. Students make meaningful and lasting connections through this work.

In this chapter I describe a 12-week thematic unit I created, with help from colleagues and the students themselves, about bread and bakeries. At the time, the entire school was conducting a "World of Work" thematic unit, so I, along with my students, chose to study bread and bakeries within that theme. I start this chapter by describing what the key elements to teaching in themes are, no matter the topic. Some of these elements include understanding children's ranges of learning, understanding the topic of study, planning curriculum, discourse, inquiry, and critique. I then share how I started the inquiry by asking the questions, What do you think you know about work? and, How are we going to learn it? After this, the chapter describes students as researchers, book authors, writers, investigators, mathematicians, historians, playwrights, inventors, community members, and workers.

What Is Needed to Teach in Theme?

First, I believe knowing each child well is key. For example, knowing how children learn at, below, and above their age range in various ways is essential. It is important to recognize that children are not empty vessels needing to be filled but, rather, citizens who bring a great deal of knowledge and are worth hearing. How I think of myself is just as important as how I think of the children I teach. I start with the ideas listed below. These help me form the kind of community that thrives when I teach in theme.

I Think of Myself as Someone Who

- Asks questions
- Listens
- Values actualizing children's ideas
- Believes in the importance of inquiry
- Is a real-life problem-solver
- Implements vocabulary and discourse
- Understands each child well
- Builds trusting environments
- Incorporates critique
- Values group work, as well as working individually
- Uses voting for decisionmaking
- Plays

Planning Versus Emergent Curriculum

One of my biggest struggles as a teacher is finding the balance between planning a curriculum and allowing curricula to emerge from students' interests. Before coming to Mission Hill School, I was used to working in a setting where everything we studied was emergent. At first, it felt imposing to me and to the students that the curriculum was decided for us. I realize that this may sound strange if the reader is in a setting where the teacher is told what to teach for every subject, which is generally the case in most schools.

At the Mission Hill School, while the topics are the same schoolwide, teachers create their curricula within the schoolwide theme. Teachers are trusted to know the material and thought of as capable curriculum developers. So each year I was planning three 3-month long thematic units. As I grew as a teacher, and gained a deeper understanding of children, I realized that there doesn't have to be one or the other. I realized that all children need interesting things to study. It was up to me to plan a thematic unit that was multidisciplinary and would introduce the children to something they may not have had experience with.

A visitor to my classroom at the Mission Hill School would see evidence of a thematic unit. He or she would also see things that might not go with the theme. There is room for creating replicas of bread in our art studio during the bakery unit, as well as drawings of still life flowers, for example.

I found that when I planned well, knew the material well, and was prepared for many possibilities, then that was when the magic would happen. I had to know what the students needed to learn. I had to know what the big ideas were for them. I did not have to have only one way to teach it, but did at least have to have one way to teach it. I had to collect as much data as I could. I took pictures and used video cameras and voice recorders.

All these tools helped me to capture students' thinking. When you know your students well, you know the importance of having their ideas actualized. I did have a lot of help getting to this place of understanding. One recommendation is working with another colleague. Having people to bounce ideas off of proved key to my success.

One of the biggest supports I had when starting to teach in themes, along with all my colleagues, was an ally and mentor named Judith Gold. As I planned for my "World of Work" theme Judith helped me to think about three key areas that I wanted children to understand about work when the theme was finished. These three things helped me to focus and frame my planning.

Three areas to guide me:

The tools—the equipment. This helped me to focus on what people use to help them do their jobs.

The jobs—the people. This was to guide me to think about how people know what they know. Did they learn from a family member or from school, or did they apprentice to learn their craft?

The food—the classroom as a place of preparation for baking. How can I arrange the room so it will serve as a place to read about bread, bake bread, and experiment with yeast?

Judith, along with other colleagues, helped me to think beyond boundaries that I did not know I had created for myself. She helped me think about fieldtrips and resources. She helped me to think through what I would need to have a bakery. One of the key pieces of advice she gave me was "[The children] are going bake everything and then you are going to freeze it." So the children made everything we sold in our bakery and froze it in my freezer. I thought I was cheating, until I realized many bakeries do the same thing. She was that person who thought anything was possible and I could make it happen.

We met and started planning months in advance. It is essential to have the time to put the pieces together. I had to plan the fieldtrips, order the books, invite guests in, and lay out what the upcoming months would look like. Two books that helped me were *Baking Bread with Children* by Warren Lee Cohen and *Loaves of Fun* by Elizabeth M. Harbison.

Research on Bakeries: Trips, Books, and Kneading the Dough!

I wrote this column for the school newsletter toward the beginning of our unit:

This week our class walked to our local Stop and Shop [grocery store]. We went to investigate their bread aisle and to visit their bakery. The students took time to look at all the different kinds of bread they sold. Many of the loaves were familiar to the children. The children were fascinated by the variety of breads. They discovered new breads. Joliana said, "I saw bread with peanuts and raisins and bread you bake at home." Arianny shared, "They had little muffins and big muffins."

I asked the children to share what they had learned from Christina the bakery manager. Jolie shared, "The only cakes they bake are birthday cakes, Thanksgiving cakes, and New Year's cakes." Jovanni also remembered they made cakes at a warehouse. Victoria said, "Someone comes at night. They put the dough in the freezer, then the next day they put it in the proofer and then in the oven." Cyrus followed with "They freeze their dough and then unfreeze it so it will last longer."

We also met two new friends stacking the shelves. Doug and Paul worked for the bread companies. Joliana asked, "Do you bake the bread?" Paul said, "No. The bread is made at a factory and I pick it up in the morning and bring it to the store and put it on the shelf."

The children spent a great day learning about all the work associated with the bakery and the bread at the Stop and Shop.

When we started this theme, I posed to the class this question: What do you think work is? Students responded by listing the following tasks: reading, cleaning, writing, homework, planting, gardening, building, learning, cooking, playing games, art, teaching, helping others.

We had many conversations about adult work and kid work. Can they be the same? Some children weren't sure, while others had strong views. One child said, opposing the idea that they could be the same, "Like construction, you could get hurt with a hammer." Another child commented back, "Yeah, but a grown-up could teach you how to use it and then it could be safe." This controversy seemed to push their ideas about work. We then talked about how both grown-ups and children do writing, do math, study history, create art, build things, and cook. It was clear that connections were starting to be made. I mentioned to them that one of the ideas about work they had mentioned was cooking. This was not a surprise, since we cook many times a week in the class.

WHAT WE LEARNED

On a trip I made independently to the North End neighborhood of Boston, I stumbled into a new bakery called Bricco Panetteria. I grabbed a business card. A week later I called Ben Tock, the head baker. I explained that we were studying bread and bakeries. I told him that we were not having luck with bakeries letting us visit. Ben went above and beyond to welcome us and teach us about bread baking. When I took the entire class to the bakery I broke the students into two groups. Ben took half the class and taught them as if they were his apprentices. He showed us the ovens, the mixers, and all the other equipment. He described the ingredients he used and where he got them from. He also spoke with the children about how he learned about how the other bakers learned as well. The students got to work with dough and made the kind of bread they sell at the bakery. (No worries—the bread the children made did not make it to the bakery's shelves!)

The other half of the class traveled with me to visit other bakeries in the area. We would walk into one, buy a few snacks, and draw in our sketchbooks as we ate. Children noticed what was sold, how the store was laid out, who was working, and what the signs said on the walls. One baker was so excited we were opening our own bakery that they bought us cupcakes.

When we arrived in a bakery employees always seemed happy to see us, especially if we bought something. But if I called ahead and said I wanted to come on a fieldtrip, most people were not accommodating. This is why I am so thankful for Ben. While the children baked with him, they asked him questions like, Where did you learn to make bread?

Making Bread

At various times during this unit, I asked children how they thought bread was made. I could have just brought out a cookbook and told them, but I wanted every aspect of study to be a learning moment. The children as a group brainstormed how they thought bread was made. Sometimes, when teaching young children, the hardest part is keeping a straight face. When they share their ideas you don't want to laugh because you are encouraging them to make guesses about what they think they know. For example, when guessing how to make bread they say, "a teaspoon of flour and a cup of salt." I turn to the board and write, "a teaspoon of flour and a cup of salt." I write it exactly the way they say it, to validate their ideas. They brainstorm; I write.

I then take the words that children say and make them into a how-to book that would be easy for us to follow as we make our first loaf of bread. We follow the children-created recipe book verbatim. The children then see the batter before it goes into the oven and after it comes out. The last time we did this the children made something kind of, sort of, looking similar to bread. We first looked at it. They each got to choose one word to describe how it looked. "Crusty." "Brown." "Bready." These were some words that were shared. Then we tasted it and used one word to describe how it tasted. Some examples were "salty," "good," and "bad."

After tasting the first loaf, the class agreed that it was "not bread." I asked how we were going to learn to make bread. "Look in books," "Look in cookbooks," "Go on the Internet," and "Ask someone to come teach us," were some of the replies. One child said, "My grandma bakes bread; she can teach us." In this process of questioning, hypothesizing, and trying things out, we practiced language arts, art, science, and mathematics. It also helped the children to understand that baking is scientific, complex, and experimental.

Transforming the Classroom

The more we read and discussed bread and bakeries, the more students wanted to know. They wanted to change our dramatic play area into a

Documenting our first loaves of bread

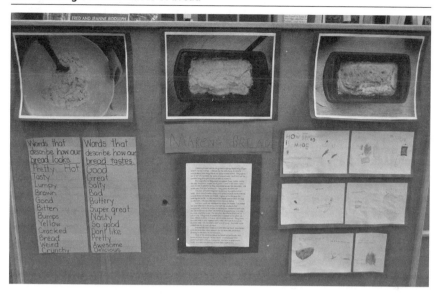

bakery. My student teacher worked with the children to think about what they would need and how they would change things around. They made lists of things, such as bowls, spoons, and trays. When they wanted play food we suggested they make it. The art studio in our classroom became an area in which to make baguettes, rolls, and pita breads. Throughout the room there were books about bread. Children would look through them to get inspired. They would hold up a picture and ask, "What's that?" After they wanted to know a particular type of bread I would go to Boardmaker. Boardmaker is a program that was designed for children who are non-verbal. I have found it to be useful for all the children in my class. It has a bank of drawings of a variety of things. I find the picture I want and glue it onto a sentence strip. The children then write the word of the type of bread. We started to create a wall of bread and bakery terms that all had pictures to go with them. This then became a resource for students while they were writing in their daily journals.

Experiments with Warm and Boiling-Hot Water

We used cookbooks to help us become better bakers. One thing that I noticed was when one is working with yeast the cookbooks always said to use warm water. The children wondered about that as well. If students didn't question it, then it would be a perfect place for me to say, "You know, I keep reading that we need warm water with the yeast; why do you think that is?" It really is an elaborate dance—encouraging students to lead their own learning, while I push their curiosity and provide resources and opportunities for them to explore and learn more deeply about the chosen topic.

We decided to conduct an experiment. We made two loaves of bread using the same recipe. With one loaf we used warm water with the yeast and with the other loaf we used boiling water. The comparative question I asked was "Will the bread made with the warm water rise more than the bread made with the boiling water?" And "Which baguette did you like better?" The children made predictions and recorded their guesses. After the bread was finished baking the students collected data about the taste. Each child had a chance to try a piece of the bread made with warm water and hot water.

Which Baguette Did You Like?

XXXXXXX	XXX	XXXX
Bread made with warm water	Bread made with hot water	They taste the same Warm = Hot

Incorporating Language Arts

Language arts is one of the first things I connect with teaching in theme. There are so many different kinds of children's books and if I discover that I want more than what is available, children can build the class library by writing them. One of the first things I do is go to Amazon and enter in the subject. Often, the books I am looking for are at the public library or in our school library. Below is a list of books in which children can find material about bread and bakeries.

Easy Readers

Bread by Joy Cowley
Wheat by Susan Canizares and Pamela Chanko
The Bakery by Frances Lee
What's Cooking? A Cookbook for Kids by Disney Book Group
The Fantastic Cake by Joy Cowley
Bread Bread Bread by Ann Morris
The Gingerbread Man by Madeline Beasley and Christine Young
The Little Red Hen by Vicki Smillie McHoull
The Little Red Hen by Janelle Cherrington

Stories

Plants We Use by Judith Hodge
A Day in the Life of a Chef by Liza Burby
Grains to Bread by Inez Snyder

The Gingerbread Man by Jim Aylesworth
The Tortilla Factory (in English and in Spanish) by Gary Paulson
Froggy Bakes a Cake by Jonathan London
Bread Bakery by Catherine Anderson
The Sleeping Bread by Stefan Czernecki and Timothy Rhodes
Tony's Bread by Tomie dePaola
Walter the Baker by Eric Carle
Bread Is for Eating by David and Phillis Gershator
Bread and Jam for Frances by Russell Hoban
Everybody Eats Bread by Diana Noonan
All About Bread by Geoffrey Patterson

During this theme students wrote journal entries of their choice; they sometimes wrote answers to questions that I posed and learned songs and poems, and we wrote books of our own. We wrote thank you cards to various people, such as employees at bakeries whom we met, and we created signs for our in-class bakery. We made posters with all the information advertising the bakery. During this theme we wrote books titled *How Bread Is Made*; *How to Make Strawberry Jam* (inspired by *Bread and Jam for Frances*); and *The Little Red Hen, Retold*.

How to Make Strawberry Jam
By the Parachuting Snails Class

Get strawberries.
Wash the strawberries.
Cut the strawberries and put them in a big bowl.
Mash the strawberries.
Squeeze the lemons.
Put them (the strawberries) in the pot.
Put in the stuff that looks like yeast but is not yeast. It's pectin.
Put in the sugar.
Get some glass jars.
Put the jam in the jars with a special tool.
Put them on the stove with the water and the thing sucks the air out like this: *sssssssssss.*
Let it sit in the pot for a while.
Pick up the jars with a special tool.
You eat it. Eat it up. Yum. Yum.
Make a sandwich.

I read aloud books about work, bread, and bakeries. A great read-aloud book about work was written by the middle school students at Mission Hill. It is titled *A Place for Me in the World*. Children read to other children.

Older students came and were book buddies in the class. We read poems and the books we had written. We read and wrote recipes. There were multiple ways for children to find information about the topic.

After we returned from visiting bakeries, children could use their sketchbooks to re-create the bakery in the block area. The block area became a diorama of the bakery. Students used blocks, found objects, tissue paper, clay, paper, and pencils to make it. They used the clay to make all the food; the blocks to make walls, doorways, and counters; and the paper and pencils to make "open" and "closed" signs, exit signs, and bathroom signs. We studied about the roles bread has played in history. Students made connections to the ancient civilizations we had learned about in the past. We also learned geography. We looked at different breads they sold in different parts of the world and how many of those breads they sold at our local grocery store. We learned about how baking is similar and different from other lines of work, from visiting other classes in the school that were studying different jobs and by hearing about them at our weekly whole-school assembly, called Friday Share.

THE LITTLE RED HEN AND MISSION HILL SCHOOL'S HABITS OF MIND

The story of *The Little Red Hen* has become a staple during our thematic unit. I originally chose the book because the hen in the story bakes a loaf of bread. I soon came to realize that the book was a true asset. It taught the children how wheat grows and about grinding wheat into flour, friendship and sharing, and learning lessons. I also used it to teach about title, author, character, and setting. At first, I started by reading two different versions of the story. We then made a Venn diagram comparing the two. I soon realized there are over 20 different versions of *The Little Red Hen*. We then made a chart to collect information.

Title	Author	Characters	Baked	Shared

As I read aloud various versions of the story, I asked students to pay close attention to who the character would be. We would make predictions about what we thought the Little Red Hen would bake and then record what she baked and check to see if she shared or didn't share with her friends.

As we talked about the Little Red Hen's sharing I had a chance to incorporate Mission Hill's habit of mind called Viewpoint. We discussed how the Little Red Hen felt when her friends didn't help and why they thought she didn't want to share. Some of the children did not like that the hen did not share. The class decided we were going to rewrite the story. In their version, when the bread is finished baking and the all the hen's friends want to have some bread the hen lets them know how she felt when they didn't help. The friends then said, "What can we do to make you feel better? The hen replies, "Next time you need to help." The friends agreed. The hen then shares the bread.

The children were also inspired to grind wheat using a mill, which I was able to acquire. We looked closely at the wheat as we put it through the mill. We used "describing words" to describe the flakes of wheat berries. We discovered that it took about five times through the mill to look like flour. A book also inspired us to grow wheat as well. It is difficult to do, so I would suggest reading about it before trying it out.

Little Red Hen Books

The Little Red Hen and the Passover Matzah by Leslie Kimmelman
The Little Red Hen by Jerry Pinkney
The Little Red Hen by Paul Galdone
The Little Red Hen by Diane Muldrow
The Little Red Hen by Lucina McQueen
The Little Red Hen: An Old Fable by Heather Forest
With Love, Little Red Hen by Alma Flor Ada
Help Yourself, Little Red Hen! by Alvin Granowsky
The Little Red Hen (Makes a Pizza) by Philemon Sturges

Opening a Bakery

Here is a column that I wrote in the school newsletter toward the end of our thematic unit on bread and bakeries:

Our Bread and Bakery unit is making both our minds and our tummies joyous. Learning different aspect of bread baking and bakery running has found a fondness for each of the children. They have worked at building a pretend bakery in our dramatic play area and are very enthusiastic about it.

I asked them, "Would you like to open a real bakery?" Every child in the class said, "yes." They didn't even let me ask another question. "We need tables!" one student yelled out. "Kathy, can we sell cake?" another asked. "We need to make posters and make an announcement at Friday Share," came more advice.

I pointed out to them that they were thinking like people who were starting a business. I told them that they were starting to think about the decor and how the bakery should look and be set up. I also pointed out that another group could think about what we sold. They said, "Bread." The other thing I told them I heard was an advertising group. They got excited about all the ways they could let people know about the bakery.

We are currently in discussions about the name for our bakery. We have some very interesting possibilities. "Ninja Bakery," "The Parachuting Snails Bakery," "The Baguette Bakery," and "Jhayden's Bakery" are just a few. We will keep you posted on what we decided and when our grand opening will be.

In a discussion with the children during one morning meeting three major groups emerged: the decor group, the "what are we selling?" group, and the advertising group. Most children found themselves interested in one particular group, while a couple of children really wanted to be in two. These groups were interest groups, so students could participate in any group they liked, but once they picked a group or groups they were considered committed to working on that team.

The Decor Group

All the children and I had visited many bakeries. We saw bakeries with walk-up counters as well as bakeries with seats for customers. When I gathered the class together on the rug I knew that they had a variety of ideas about the kind of bakery they wanted, but I also knew they all had visited at least three bakeries during our field trips. I asked the children, "What do we need to set up the bakery?" As the students shared their ideas I wrote them on a whiteboard so the children could see. One of the first ideas that a student shared was that she wanted tables and chairs. We discussed it and the children agreed it would be an eat-in bakery. Another student connected with this idea. She wanted to make sure that we had different-sized tables for different-sized people. She said, "We will have grown-ups and little kids coming." Another child remembered that one of the bakeries had "cash only" signs. "We need those," she said. Another student said, "We need a tip jar." A student said, "What's that?" The first replied, "If you do a good job, people give you money." The team was excited to add a tip jar.

We needed a sign. We needed tablecloths. We needed an "open" and "closed" sign. Once our initial brainstorm was complete we started to get to work. I gave them three-fourths of the classroom to transform into the bakery. The reason they didn't have the whole class was because when the bakery would be open the children would have shifts. When students were not working in the bakery they were working on other projects in the class.

We started to move bookshelves around to make barriers so customers could not go behind the counters. The children then started looking for tables of different heights. They also found chairs of different heights to go with each table. They asked the 4th- and 5th-grade teacher if they could borrow some tablecloths. They knew the teacher might have them because he always had tablecloths for the students to work on. Sure enough, James lent them his tablecloths. We had also been experimenting with trying to grow wheatgrass. The students placed the planters with three and four little wheatgrass sprouts on each table.

One group started the art project of making the sign. The sign was made out of felt. In an earlier class discussion, the class had decided on the name for the bakery. The decor group started the work. I wrote out the name of the bakery on a piece of paper. I asked the children to count the letters. We needed one felt square for each letter. "I need to know how many felt squares to cut," I told them. Once I got the figure, I started cutting. The students had a say in the colors of felt that were used for the sign. The students then started to draw and cut out felt letters that later were glued onto the squares.

The students continued to work on different signs for the bakery. One last area that they set up was the working/serving area behind the counter. I recommended that they make sure there were tables back there for baking and holding extra baked goods. They put together two rectangle tables.

The Advertising Group

"We need to make an announcement at Friday Share." A student shared. Families and visitors often attend as well. It is a great time to make an announcement about a new bakery opening. The children wanted to advertise it in our school newsletter, make signs advertising the bakery, and go to each classroom to announce that the bakery would be coming.

I asked the group, "What do you want people to know about the bakery?" Children replied, "We want people to know where it is," "We want to tell them when they can come," "We should tell them it is cash only," and "I want them to know what kinds of things we will sell." As they presented and shared to our community about the bakery, they took turns telling about different aspects of the bakery.

The "What Do We Want to Sell?" Group

This group brainstormed ideas about what they wanted to sell. Like the other groups, they reported back to the whole class so that the class knew what they were thinking and could add more things as well. The students included almost all the breads that we had made previously in the class. They added pumpkin bread and banana bread. They really liked the cheese bread, so we included that as well. The children wanted to sell cake and cupcakes as well. I could have argued and said that we would be making

Welcome sign for our bakery

only nutritious items for the bakery. I could have steered them to focus on just bread, but I chose to not do that. Instead, I chose to let them actualize their ideas. We did sell only a couple of slices of cake and we did make the cookies smaller than the average cookie. This group had a vision for the bakery and I really wanted to be a part of helping the vision occur. The students had also visited many bakeries where cupcakes seemed to be the center of attention.

One of the things the children wanted to sell was chocolate chip cookies. I read the book *All in Just One Cookie*, by Susan E. Goodman. In the back of the book there was a recipe. We decided to make the recipe. There was also a tub of store-bought chocolate chip cookie dough in our fridge that a parent had donated. We made batches of both cookies. I told

The bakery setup

them about a concept called market research. I told them this is where you have a product and you see how people react to it. We placed the cookies on two separate plates marked "cookie one" and "cookie two."

Stories with Recipes

Mama Panya's Pancakes by Mary Chamberlin and Rich Chamberlin
On Top of Spaghetti by Paul Brett Johnson
How to Make an Apple Pie and See the World by Marjorie Priceman
Good Enough to Eat: A Kid's Guide to Food and Nutrition by Lizzy
    Rockwell
Mr. Cookie Baker by Monica Wellington
Skillet Bread, Sourdough, and Vinegar Pie by Loretta Frances Ichord
All in Just One Cookie by Susan E. Goodman
Sun Bread by Elisa Kleven

The following is a school newsletter article I wrote about what we discovered from our market research:

"We are doing market research," Kadian said to Joanie as we walked into the office. "Want to do a taste test?" Irea asked. Joanie smiled. Ayla and Joanie stopped what they were doing to help the children in the Parachuting Snails class learn about an important part of opening a business.

Zayna said, "Try cookie one and cookie two." They both tried the cookies. Joanie said, "They are both so good, it is hard to decide." After Ayla and Joanie tried the cookies they told the group which one they liked better. "Make a tally," Rafael said to Zayna. She was holding a clipboard with a space for both cookie one and cookie two. As we went around the school Zayna tallied.

We came to Jenerra's room. Miss Jenerra is serious about her taste-testing. She tried cookie one. "This is a good dunking cookie." She tried cookie two. "Oh this is like a cloud." The children smiled. They were very serious about gathering the data they would need to make an informed decision about which cookie to sell.

We brought the cookies back to our class for a testing. I am happy to announce with a landslide cookie two won. Twenty-two people voted for cookie two and 7 people voted for cookie one.

The recipe for these cookies came from a children's book titled *All in Just One Cookie* by Susan E. Goodman. It is a wonderful book about where all the ingredients come from to make up these cookies. Luckily for you on June 5, 6, and 7 our Bakery will be open.

Our survey was a great experience for the children because it was authentic data collection. They seemed to understand why it was important and why it mattered. Often, when children collect data from scripted curriculum the data questions that are asked are irrelevant to young children. One data question I came across was "Are you a boy or a girl?" Or "What color eyes do you have?" I think these questions could be fun to answer, but the questions we ask young children do not have to be irrelevant.

Market research for cookie recipes

The group brought the findings back to the class, and the students all knew which cookie we would sell.

Jobs at the Bakery

As we visited bakeries and gathered research, the children realized that there were different jobs at bakeries, and we needed jobs at our bakery: cashier, ticket giver, seller, inventory, and manager. The children and I explained all the jobs to each other.

"The cashier gets the money," one child said. "What happens if you do not know how much to tell people?" another child interrupted. "You could ask a friend or a teacher," another child offered. "Should we have grown-ups to help us on days that the bakery is open?" I asked. "Ummm humm, yes," a child declared.

I explained that the ticket giver gave out snap cubes to each person who came to the bakery. This was our way of knowing how many people shopped at our establishment. When I first started teaching about the world of work we used tickets. I found that they were hard for the students to grasp. I discovered if we used snap cubes they were much easier to group into 10s as we counted them.

Then I gave them a piece of paper and they got to pick the top-three jobs that they wanted to do.

At the end of each day we would group by 10s, count by 10, and make a prediction for the following day. The next day we would do it all over again and then see how our predictions matched up to the actual number of people who visited the bakery. The ticket giver's job is very important because the ticket giver is the first person the customer meets.

We had two sellers on each shift. The sellers greeted customers and handed customers what they wanted. "You have to say, 'Thank you and come again,'" said a child as she described how to treat the customers. Another student said, "You have to smile and say, 'Welcome to the Parachuting Snails Bakery.'" And, of course, as one student put it, "We have to work!"

Inventory has become an important job in the bakery. We discovered that both supermarkets and bakeries kept track of their inventory. When I first started doing the bakery children would get a large piece of paper and make columns for each item we sold. During the bakery they would make tallies every time someone sold something. It was hard for the children to keep track. I did something different this year. I made the sheet for the students with 10 pictures of bananas for banana bread. Each item had 10 pictures of a piece of challah or 6 pictures of a cupcake. Children then were able to x them out and count how many were left. I went back and forth with the idea of whether I should make the inventory sheet or whether the students should make a large chart inventory record. It felt

We used snap cubes for counting customers.

uncomfortable to me because it was something that I had introduced and it was not kid created. I put it into place and it worked well. I was still uneasy. I struggle with making sure that my voice or ideas do not over-shadow those of the children.

Then there was the job of the manager. One child said, "That's the boss." "They tell you what to do," said another. "He is the king!" "Well, not exactly," I interjected. "He or she helps to make sure everyone is do-ing what they are supposed to do." I continued with a question, "What happens if you are the manager and people are not doing their jobs?" "What?" said a voice; "what?" Another child said, "The boss will yell at you." Another voice added, "You're going to lose your job." I helped them change the conversation into what everyone can do to make sure everyone shares the work. "Many hands make light work," I shared with the group. We also discussed what happens if someone is out sick or doesn't come to work. We talked about how people might have to do two jobs.

Cookbooks

More Than Graham Crackers: Nutrition Information and Food Preparation with Young Children by Nancy Wanamaker
Knead It, Punch It, Bake It: The Ultimate Breadmaking Book for Parents and Kids by Evan Jones and Judith Jones (The best book for baking with children)
The Waldorf Book of Bread by Marsha Post and Winslow Eliot

I had ordered aprons from a uniform catalog. They had to be altered, and the children worked with Ayla, our principal, and her daughter, Quela, to alter them. We then worked with Jeanne, our art teacher, to add art to the aprons. Each child's apron was unique and clearly showed the child's personality.

As the children worked at school I sent homework as well. The bakery ran for 3 days, with each day having three 30-minute shifts. It was a fantastic puzzle I needed to solve; I had to create a grid that gave each child a job each day. I sent home the grid for families so that they could come and see their children working in the bakery.

Proud bakers

Children's Reflections

I wrote the following for the school newsletter, reflecting on our bakery:

> Being metacognitively aware of one's own learning can be hard. Thinking about your thinking isn't always easy. Even though it is challenging it is something that I expect. Before our bakery doors opened I shared with the students that after their shift was finished they would need to spend time drawing and writing about their experience. They did this after each shift.
>
> Jolie shared: "Day 1: My dad came to the bakery. He got a brownie pop, a jam, a banana bread, and a red thing. Day 2: I was the ticket giver. It was kind of fun. It was kind of fun cause I had to wait a lot. Day 3: I had fun I saw all the cake got sold out."
>
> I also interviewed the children, asking them, "How did it feel to work in the bakery?" Dalia shared, "I got to work and it feels like I had a job. I was good because I got to help people. I looked at all my friends and they were happy." Arianny shared that she was nervous because she was worried when she was passing out the cupcakes she would mess up the frosting.
>
> Rafael said, "At the bakery I gave food to the people." He went on to share how he felt: "It was so much fun to me because I love going to the bakery."
>
> We also kept a count of how many visitors we had to the bakery each day. On the first day we had 45 people. On the second we had 55. And on the third day we had 75 people. Each day we wondered about how many visitors we had the day before and if more people would come, fewer people would come, or the same amount of people would come. Our predications were very close.

Reflection is an important part of any thematic unit. It is important to note that reflection is something that should be happening throughout the entire theme. It is important to have children think about their thinking as they are working through it. Written reflection is important, but so is verbal reflection. This is another reason why forming a community in which discourse is something that the children are used to and participate in will help them to listen to others as well as formulate their own ideas. I mix up our written and verbal reflections.

One day I may pose a question such as "What do you think you know about work?" Or "What did you learn about bread and bakeries that you didn't know before?" I will then have the children go off, think about it, and then record their ideas through pictures and writing. After the children have done that, we will come back together.

And they will share their work. I mark out a time each day for children to share their learning.

Another way I approach reflection is that I pose a question and write down each child's name and then what he or she says next to it. Not every child has to share. Listening to other children is often a jumping-off point for children to understand and form their own reflections.

CONCLUSION

Reflection is a key part of my learning as I teach in theme. I have taught the "World of Work" theme four times. Each time the cycle comes around again I think about how I will plan for it. Even though I have taught it before, I look at it through new eyes. I think about what worked well and what I could do better. I also think about how I can make sure I honor the emergence of students' ideas as they unfold. I revisit what I want the children to know when the theme is over.

As we start the theme I continue reflecting on how things are going. I use the opportunity each week to write a column for our school newsletter. This is a place for me to publicly reflect on where the children are in their learning and where we can go.

This year there were many elements that we had covered in the past that came back again. They were a part of the planning that I had done. There were many elements that I had not planned for, elements that emerged and that the children led the learning on. As this happened I needed to be aware of the learning that was happening.

I walked away this year feeling very proud of the young people I taught. They used their voices to share ideas with their other classmates and myself.

CHAPTER 4

The Impact of Nature and Play

Geralyn Bywater McLaughlin

It was hard to get the pretending into me. Once I did, it felt great.

—Student, 1st grade

Impact. When I think about a successful curriculum, I think about the impact it had—on teachers as well as on students. When a curriculum is powerful, the students, the teachers, and even the families can all feel a shift that occurs. In thinking over the themes to write about for this collection, I wanted to explore themes that have made an impact on me as well as on my students.

I have been an early childhood educator for 25 years and am constantly amazed at all there is still to learn about teaching young children. I am one of the founding teachers of Mission Hill School and taught all the early grades—kindergarten through 3rd grade, over the first 11 years of the school. Before that, I taught for 8 years at an independent school (preschool and kindergarten). In 2008, I took 4 years off from the classroom, and during that time I spent a year with my own sons (twins, who were 4-year-olds at the time), became a more active advocate for quality play in children's lives, started a nonprofit called Empowered by Play, coached Head Start and Early Head Start teachers, and became the director of a nonprofit project called Defending the Early Years (DEYproject.org). In 2012, I returned to Mission Hill School and resumed full-time teaching, this time with the new class for 3-year-olds.

Through all these experiences, I have seen firsthand that creating engaging curricula makes school an interesting place for both teachers and students. When the curriculum is dry and scripted it is hard for teachers and students to stay interested. I saw this when my twins went to kindergarten. There, they faced piles of meaningless worksheets and a seemingly endless series of uninspired, scripted lessons. Each day was filled with drudgery. With recess just about disappearing from their schedule, my sons plodded along, living for the two times a week they had gym class. Just about halfway through that kindergarten year one of my sons could not take it any longer. As I dropped him off at school one morning he asked, "Mom, can I retire from school?" His brother was less diplomatic and angrier. When I picked him up one Friday he got in the car and started screaming, yelling, and hitting in utter frustration.

In speaking with their teachers, who were hardworking and dedicated, I found that to a large extent their hands were tied by administrative directives—pressures from the principal. I found the teachers responsive to my concerns and my sons' frustrations, and together we found ways to bring creativity, imagination, and playful learning into the school day for the remainder of that school year. We made it through till June—barely—and for me it illustrated the utter importance of engaging and inspiring curricula.

In this chapter I will describe how one particular theme had a positive impact: "Garden Friends," a subtheme within the whole-school theme of "Natural Science." I will describe why this theme was chosen, and how it affected students, teachers, families, and the school community.

LIFE SCIENCE: GARDEN FRIENDS WITH 5-, 6-, AND 7-YEAR-OLDS

After teaching for 18 years, I thought I had learned a few things about the classroom. And perhaps I had. However, that doesn't mean I had figured everything out—far from it. One of the wonderful things about teaching is that you never quite know what each school year, each day, and each child will bring. The school year 2006–2007 was one of the most challenging I have ever experienced. The social dynamics were a constant source of stress and strife for my students, my families, my assistant teacher, and me.

The problems I encountered, mostly around the influences of popular culture, media, and the oversexualization of my students, caught me off guard and utterly unprepared. I watched my 5-year-old girls vying for the attention of the "coolest" 1st-grade boy. They would push to be near him at the sand table and would groan audibly if I didn't place them in his book group. Students in the class thought of each other as "boyfriend" and "girl-friend." Freeze dance and soul train, which are usually a big hit and lots of fun, had a new dimension as students danced out the social scenarios they had seen in music videos. My 5-, 6-, and 7-year-olds played out and talked about "being in the club" and "drinking Heineken." They wrote about the popular music world in their journals and turned the block area into a radio station and performed for each other—pretending to be the stars they'd watched in videos. At the end of a particularly frustrating day I described the situation to my principal: "We have two 'middle schools' in our school. The middle school and the K–1!" In a nutshell, that is how the year felt.

There was another aspect of this that negatively affected our classroom community, and that was the idea of certain kids' wearing the "right" sneakers. This was among a particular group of boys, but the rest of the class was affected. It was something we had class meetings about, and tried to minimize the negative effects of, but it was a continuous struggle. One morning, as they walked up the stairs to our second-floor classroom, a kindergarten boy and a 1st-grade boy got in a pushing and hitting fight because the younger boy said he was wearing Carmelo Anthonys and the older boy said, "No, those are Jordans." Another boy, whose mom refused to buy expensive sneakers, had repeated meltdowns (crying, throwing things, yelling) when other boys arrived at school with new sneakers, stylish shirts or outfits, or big plastic gold rings.

Throughout the year, I tried many strategies to counteract the negative impact that these complicated factors were having on our ability to live, learn, and laugh. Somehow we made it through. That June, when our staff met for our end-of-the-year retreat I remember sharing my struggles and my determination to get a better handle on what felt to me like a real crisis in the early childhood group. I realize that many schools handle this kind of situation by requiring students to all wear the same uniform (Mission Hill School does not require uniforms). However, the problems I am describing go beyond just the shirt and pants that are worn by students. These are just examples of ways in which the narratives and messages many students brought to school seemed to be strongly influenced by media that led to unkindness in the classroom.

My colleague Kathy Clunis D'Andrea had gone to Wheelock College and knew of a great resource there. She told me about Diane Levin, a professor there, and suggested I enroll in the 2-day summer media institute, called Media Madness: The Impact of Sex, Violence, and Commercial Culture on Children and Society. Kathy's suggestion ended up being one of the best and most transformative pieces of advice I ever received. It was in that course that I started to connect more of the dots regarding what I was seeing in the classroom. And the good news was, many of those same students would be back with me again for the following school year. I had the whole summer to plan specifically with their needs in mind and to intentionally create a curriculum that fit their needs.

As the new school year began, I knew that one huge goal was to find ways to bring back childhood—making even more time in the day for creative and imaginative play. I also wanted to encourage kids to turn off their screens and become more connected with the natural world, their classmates, and their own selves. To this end, I titled my fall curriculum unit "Garden Friends: Taking Care of Each Other and Taking Care of the

Earth." I had studied gardens with young children before, but this time I had an added goal of lessening the influence of screen messages.

Here is a column I wrote with colleagues in the *Mission Hill School News* that fall:

> "Can we dig for worms?" asked Amarn. We were in front of the school. "That's a good idea for another day," I answered. "Today we are looking." We also smelled the pink roses, rubbed the rough and smooth bark of the tree, and heard the red cardinal. We saw a spider spinning a web, a butterfly flying, a bumblebee sitting on a flower, and many more wonderful things, all in our own front yard.
>
> After looking carefully, the children took time to draw and write in their garden journals. Aneli drew a picture of the pink rose and dictated, "I have a rose in my garden. The school garden has a rose, too." Franz loved the huge orange flower in the corner of the garden. He dictated, "Dear Daddy, This flower is one of my favorite flowers in the garden. We can go into the garden that's in front of the school. Love, Franz."
>
> This fall, our school is studying natural sciences. Our focus will be around gardens. We will dig for worms, just like Amarn suggested, and try to grow our own garden inside. Stay tuned for more information as the weeks unfold. In the meantime, take a few moments with your child to explore a garden near you.
>
> —*Geralyn McLaughlin, Tanaysha Howell, & Melissa Richards*

I knew from experience that one excellent antidote to screen addiction is nature. Children are fascinated by it. It's also affordable and available, even around our urban school. We got our hands dirty and looked closely at snails, spiders, butterflies, worms, and more. Taking care of the creatures in our classroom and our school yard gave the children real work and a positive focus—right from the start. There is empathy that grows from working with creatures in nature, especially if they are smaller than you. I remember one day when I had brought my window boxes of begonias from home. It was getting colder outside, and before the plants died from a frost, I thought the students would enjoy exploring them. The students were excited. They quickly donned the gardening gloves and hand tools we kept at the ready. They began looking closely, finding dead leaves to gently pull off. Soon I heard excited squeals as they discovered a few spiders among the begonias. The students were delighted with the find and gently held the spiders for closer observation.

Every other year, in the fall, the entire Mission Hill School explores the theme of "Natural Science." Within each of the broad themes at

Mission Hill teachers choose aspects of those themes to focus on within their classrooms, chosen based on teacher preferences, available resources, and the developmental level of students, among other criteria. However, at the beginning of many of the "Natural Science" themes (although not all), the school has collectively decided to explore together the subtheme of "Monarch Butterflies." This decision was made because the lives of monarchs can be studied and explored at many developmental levels and because they seem to be naturally enthralling for young and older children alike. I led my class through an exploration of monarchs, along with the rest of the school. This theme fit in perfectly with our classroom study of "Garden Friends."

Before school even started in the fall, the staff at Mission Hill School ordered from a nonprofit organization called Monarch Watch enough monarch caterpillars for every classroom to have at least a dozen. In addition, teachers and students looked under common milkweed leaves at our staff retreat in New Hampshire, and elsewhere, for additional caterpillars. Along with the caterpillars (which were shipped in small containers sitting on a bit of jellylike nourishing food for them), Monarch Watch also sent little plastic habitats where the caterpillars could live and pupate until they were placed in a larger habitat before they broke their chrysalides and transformed into beautiful butterflies. Most teachers, using their classroom budgets or rummage sale skills, acquired a larger terrarium in which to raise their monarchs to adulthood.

As the caterpillars grew, students fed them and counted the leaves they ate. Students carefully observed the shapes the caterpillars ate into leaves, using magnifying glasses, and they drew pictures and many different representations of the insects, using a variety of media. Throughout, students asked many questions at our morning meeting and during their observations: "Why are they those colors?" "How do they see?" "Why do they have so many eyes?" "What can they see?" "How many legs do they have?" "Do they smell?" "How do they know how to form a chrysalis?" "What happens inside of the chrysalis?" "Why are they green with gold dots?" I kept track of their questions on a large piece of butcher paper at the front of the classroom and published many of their questions and observations in the *Mission Hill School News*. Students each took notes in their monarch journals, along with their drawings of the monarchs on that day. Older students carefully measured the length of the caterpillars as they grew and we all read many books and websites about caterpillars and monarchs in general. Favorites included Eric Carle's *The Very Hungry Caterpillar*; James Prosek's *Bird, Butterfly, Eel*; and Sam Swope and Sue Riddle's *Gotta Go! Gotta Go!*

Here is a column that I wrote with colleagues in the *Mission Hill School News* about our monarch study:

Do caterpillars drink? Why is milkweed called "milkweed?" Do monarch caterpillars have two heads? (It looks like they do!)

These are just a few of the many questions asked by our 5-, 6-, and 7-year-olds. To find out the answers to our questions, we are observing our caterpillars closely, reading books about Monarchs and talking to people in other classrooms (one of the benefits of our shared curriculum!). Some of our questions we will be able to find answers to, but other questions might just keep us wondering. Monarchs have been fascinating scientists for a very long time, and there remain many secrets to the amazing insects. Besides, isn't wondering wonderful?

This week, we have been wondering how long it will take our pupae to hatch into butterflies. We've made predictions and are keeping track of the days. Making predictions about time is a tricky task for 5-, 6-, and 7-year-olds. They are still learning about days, weeks, and months, and how long each of these are. As we keep track of the days, we will have solid evidence (one of our Mission Hill habits of mind) to answer our question. We won't have to wonder too long about this one!

How long do you think it will take for our butterflies to hatch? Make your own predictions at home, and stay tuned for our data results.

Finally, we are still planning on taking our field trip to the Butterfly Place next week, Thursday, October 2nd. Remember to send a lunch that day (unless you get free lunch) and to be on time for school. We are asking families to contribute $5.00 toward the cost of the trip. Thank you!

—Geralyn McLaughlin and Jada Brown,
Kathy Clunis and Lindsey Rieder

One of the many unique and wonderful aspects of monarchs is that they migrate to a particular region in Mexico every winter. Actually, not every specimen migrates, since most monarchs have a life span of just a few weeks. But, somehow, the caterpillars that are born in October (or thereabouts, in Massachusetts) know that they need to fly hundreds of miles south to Mexico. There are so many fascinating questions to explore with children about this process:

1. How does a caterpillar that looks like a worm turn into something completely different? What happens inside that chrysalis?
2. Where is Mexico? (we conduct rather in-depth explorations of maps—as well as cultural explorations of Mexico, especially the

important cultural role monarchs play in the state of Michoacán in Mexico, where the monarchs from the eastern part of the United States migrate).

3. How does such a tiny insect fly so far? (What does the scientific base of knowledge tell us about how this is possible—such as the ability of monarchs to "float" on pockets of south-heading winds?) With this question, as with others, there are genuine mysteries and questions that students can ask, right alongside professional biologists!

4. How do monarch butterflies navigate? (This has connections to other animals and birds—how do they know where to migrate? Do they have an internal GPS?)

5. Why do they migrate to this particular place in Mexico? What are the particular features of this region (mountains, temperate climate, particular kinds of trees—pine-oak forests)?

6. Will this region always be there for the monarchs? Is it okay that these trees are being cut down in large numbers? What would happen if most of the trees were cut down and replaced with houses and other buildings?

7. Why is it that there are such wildly fluctuating numbers of monarchs in Mexico from winter to winter?

8. How might the phenomenon of fluctuating monarch numbers be related to global warming? What causes global warming?

9. Are pesticides killing monarchs? What is the effect of pesticides on monarch populations?

Questions like these were not only raised in my classroom but could also be found posted on the walls throughout the school, deepening our sense of immersion and community learning.

In October, after almost all our caterpillars had already metamorphosed into butterflies, the entire school put together a "going away" celebration for our butterflies. From the youngest children to the oldest, we gathered on the school yard with our classrooms and with butterflies in hand. Many students had created specially made monarch-themed artwork. Some held posters that read "Have a nice trip!" or "Be careful!" Many students had made monarch-themed hats or headdresses. Students were surprisingly quiet as poems and stories about monarchs were read aloud, and then the butterflies were set free. It is tempting for children to chase butterflies flying around them, but they resisted. The containers in which the butterflies were raised were left out with the butterflies, and in due time, they flew away from us, never to be seen by us again.

Of course, there were also other—perhaps unintended—lessons as well. What is death? Why did some of the caterpillars not come out of their chrysalis? Why do insects live such short lives? But on the other side of the coin—how do so many of them survive, despite what seem to be small, fragile bodies within a hostile world, where birds and other animals might view them as a tasty snack? Why do they have such bold colors while so many other animals are camouflaged by their appearance? And so many other questions remain—why do the butterflies stop eating common milkweed in adulthood? How does the milkweed protect the caterpillars and butterflies with nutrients that are poisonous to other animals? How does a monarch's proboscis work? And on and on . . .

After our study of the monarchs, we turned our focus back to gardens and the many living things that can grow there. One book that is central to this curriculum is *Garden Friends* by DK Publications. The book has beautiful photographs of about a dozen different creatures you can find in the garden. The science vocabulary is there—through easy-to-read labels of the creatures and their various features. The students gravitate to the clear and colorful close-ups of spiders, snails, dragonflies, worms, and more. The photographs and background knowledge from the book gave our outdoor observations and investigations a deep level of engagement. The students felt a connection to the spiders, snails, and worms we found in our school yard gardens, after reading about them in our book. The book is also accessible on many levels. Nonreaders and readers alike can appreciate the photographs and information. I had eight copies of the book, and they were in constant use.

The book has a social-emotional component as well, as each creature is identified and recognized for something unique in a friendly way: "Hello, Spider, you are . . ." Such an approach models beautifully the way that we can recognize and appreciate the uniqueness of each other. It led to a major experience during this curriculum—the creation of our own classroom book—inspired by *Garden Friends*. Each day, we would draw one student's name out of a can. For that day, we would collectively share good thoughts about that child—focusing on what the child was good at, what he or she liked to do, or other characteristics we had observed. The focus was not on the physical characteristics but, rather, on the kind of person the child was. I wanted the students to understand that everyone in our classroom community had something valuable to offer us, and that it is important to include everyone. As each student shared a positive thought about the focus student for the day, I recorded the ideas on a big chart for everyone to see. After every student had a chart filled with positive reflections about him or her, the student had the chance to pick one of those items to illustrate for our class book, such as "Hello, Laneah, you love to read." In the end, we had copies of our class book for every student to keep.

I have continued to use the *Garden Friends* book and the theme in my classroom. This past year, with my 3-year-olds and young 4-year-olds, I used the book to propel us deep into caring for living things and each other. This year the snails were what the class really gravitated to:

wanting to bring the snails in from the school yard, create a habitat, and care for them. We researched what snails need in their habitat and then took turns taking care of them. Many students truly grasped the concept of keeping the habitat damp and took very seriously the job of spraying the snails with water. We made a class book about our snails and even made a presentation to the whole school at Friday Share about how to care for snails. The students brainstormed ideas and we made charts—illustrated with photos—which we hung in the classroom so that anyone who came in could see how we care for each other, the snails, our class turtle, and our fish. Intentionally slowing things down so that you can spend time getting dirty, experiencing nature, and doing the real work of figuring out how to care for living things (including each other) always makes for valuable time—especially in our current fast-paced, media-filled world.

NATURE AND PLAY—FINDING TIME EVERY DAY

Bringing both nature and imaginative play into the classroom have become central to my teaching. I continually strive to include opportunities for students to imagine, pretend, and play. In part I design units to celebrate and highlight children's ability to be in charge of their own learning as they create stories, invent problems, and evolve as powerful individuals. I want all students to know that pretend play is important and to practice making choices that involve imagining, pretending, and playing. They learn how to create their own entertainment and that many things can be used for play—rocks, sticks, dirt, cardboard boxes, scraps of fabric, unmatched socks. In 2007, I chose this curriculum specifically for this particular group of students to help counteract the media influences that had turned much of their free play into scripted play (acting out what they saw on the screen, instead of what was in their own imagination). Once I recognized the positive impact that this curriculum had on my students in 2007 I continued to keep it as a part of what I do.

That year, we focused our literacy work on reading stories that celebrate imagination, such as *Amazing Grace* by Mary Hoffman, *Gilberto and the Wind* by Marie Hall Ets, and *Roxaboxen* by Alice McLerran. I found related poems to recite and songs to sing. I found that by reading the books—with examples of imaginative play, especially play in nature—and with natural props I was able to give my students excellent role models to emulate. Many of the children who are depicted in the TV shows, videos, and movies that my students were watching are not good examples of creative, imaginative players. After reading a book, such as *Gilberto and the Wind*, we would go right outside and I could see the students trying out the play that Gilberto had enjoyed in the book. After reading *Roxaboxen*, students began using natural materials to start building little homes—much like they had seen in the story.

For the first time, I included playing outside on our project time choice board—so that small groups of children could spend more time outdoors. I also brought dolls and other housekeeping props outside—something that seems so natural but that I had never done. As they played, I saw students who were stressed and often noncompliant become more playful and relaxed—as they invented running games or hugged a baby doll as they sat under a tree. One student, who had been in a family crisis much of the year, made herself her very own "buddy"—a life-sized friend made from a carpet tube and other recycled materials that she hugged, played with, and proudly carried around.

The students had special journals to record and reflect in about their play each day. I had students practice describing how they felt while they were engaged in their chosen activity. I observed closely as the children played—making notes and taking photographs. I made bulletin boards in the classroom to document the work of their play.

On one bulletin board I also shared with families a quote from Susan Linn's *The Case for Make Believe: Saving Play in a Commercialized World* to help illustrate my curriculum decisions: "The ability to play is central to our capacity to take risks, to experiment, to think critically, to act rather than react, to differentiate ourselves from our environment, and to make life meaningful" (2008, p. 41).

One student stands out in my mind—Antoine (pseudonym). In his early years, Antoine had been exposed to a great deal of popular media. He was tuned in to the teenage/grown-up world and had trouble making friends his own age. I struggled to find ways for him to be comfortable and happy at school. During this curriculum he found some of his happiest school moments. He used recycled materials to build his own skate park and used found objects (boxes and bottles) to make his own drum set. Antoine worked on and perfected these projects over a number of weeks. Toward the end of the curriculum I sat with him for a reflective interview. I asked, "What are three words that describe you at school?" He paused and then said, "I feel good, I feel safe, and I feel happy." As his teacher, who had seen Antoine struggle for 2 years to feel comfortable and trusting at school, I could feel in that moment the power of his calm confidence and the power of this curriculum. I asked Antoine what he liked about our curriculum and he replied, "I was pretending I was downtown. I had the bass drum, the solo drum, and the high drum." He added, "It was hard to get the pretending into me. Once I started, I felt good."

His words had a deep impact on me. From that moment on, I knew that I had to become a stronger advocate for imaginative play. I saw the transformation that this student had made. I knew it was the culmination of 2 years of hard work—on his part and mine—to build trust in him and in me. And I saw that the explicit focus on transforming his imitative play of pop culture icons, which often left him feeling edgy and unsettled, into imaginative play, where he was in control as he created his own story, led to a tremendous change. I understood that a child could become empowered by play.

CONCLUSION

I began teaching in 1989. Since then, I have come to deeply understand that experiences with nature and time for play belong at school. Through my first 18 years of teaching I observed a dramatic shift in how young children play. It was through my work with Professor Diane Levin and the Media Madness Institute at Wheelock College that I learned that many others had been aware of the shift. They, too, were working hard to counteract the negative impact that media and other cultural influences were having on young children and that have led to the worrisome decline in play. This shift has been documented by many researchers, including Peter Gray. He writes:

> Over the past half century, in the United States and other developed nations, children's free play with other children has declined sharply. Over the same period, anxiety, depression, suicide, feelings of helplessness, and narcissism have increased sharply in children, adolescents, and young adults. This article documents these historical changes and contends that the decline in play has contributed to the rise in the psychopathology of young people. Play functions as the major means by which children (1) develop intrinsic interests and competencies; (2) learn how to make decisions, solve problems, exert self-control, and follow rules; (3) learn to regulate their emotions; (4) make friends and learn to get along with others as equals; and (5) experience joy. Through all of these effects, play promotes mental health. (Gray, 2011, p. 443)

My work with young children, and with Antoine in particular, has profoundly affected me—propelling me to become a vocal advocate for play in children's lives—at home and at school. It has been life changing, in fact. My "aha" moment with Antoine happened 8 years ago and since that time I have talked with just about everyone I know about the importance of quality play in young children's lives. While living in New York I started Empowered by Play, to help families and teachers protect and promote imaginative play in our way too busy, media-filled, consumer-driven world. I write and speak about play whenever I can. Now, being back in the classroom full time, I see how my classroom has evolved from my first classroom 25 years ago. I currently make a conscious effort to keep media-linked books and toys out of my classroom. I know that children are bombarded with commercials when they are not in school—and

I want to keep my classroom a commercial-free space. I use open-ended natural materials (pine cones, wood cookies, etc.) instead of plastic food in my pretend corner, propelling students to use their imaginations even more. I work on ways to bring nature inside and to maximize our time spent outside. As I build relationships with families, I talk with them about screen time, outdoor-play time, and experiences with nature and natural materials. And when families ask, I have many more resources at my fingertips about the benefits of play and playful learning.

At this point in my career I think, yes, I have learned a few things. I now know that giving children quality play experiences in nature and with simple, open-ended props will make a profound impact on them and their learning.

Author's note: Parts of this chapter were originally published in the magazine *Rethinking Schools* in the Spring 2009 edition. Since then, *Rethinking Schools* has included it in three of their collections: *Rethinking Popular Culture and Media* (2011), *Rethinking Elementary Education* (2012), and the forthcoming *Rethinking Sexism, Gender, and Sexuality* (Spring 2015).

RESOURCES

Allen, J., & Humphries, T. (2003). *Are you a snail?* Madison, WI: Demco Media.

Carle, E. (1994). *The very hungry caterpillar.* New York, NY: Philomel.

DK Publishing. (2003). *Garden friends.* New York, NY: Darling Kindersley.

Prosek, J. (2008). *Bird, butterfly, eel.* New York, NY: Simon & Schuster.

Swope, S. & Riddle, S. (2000). *Gotta go, gotta go!* New York, NY: Farrar, Straus and Giroux.

Children's Stories with Imaginative Play

Ajmera, M., & Ivanko, J.D. (2001). *Come out and play.* Watertown, MA: Charlesbridge.

Ets, M. H. (1978). *Gilberto and the wind.* New York, NY: Puffin Books.

Hoffman, M. (1991). *Amazing Grace.* New York, NY: Dial Books for Young Readers.

McLerran, A. (1991). *Roxaboxen.* New York, NY: HarperCollins.

McPhail, D. (1984). *Fix-it.* New York, NY: Picture Puffin.

Ryan, P. M. (2002). *Mud is cake.* New York, NY: Hyperion.

General Resources

Arnold, J. (2014). *Their name is Today: Reclaiming childhood in a hostile world.* Walden, NY: Plough.

Gray, P. (2011). The decline of play and the rise of psychopathology in young children and adolescents. *American Journal of Play, 3*(4), 443–463.

Levin, D. (2013). *Beyond remote-controlled childhood: Teaching young children in the media age*. Washington, DC: National Association for the Education of Young Children.

Levin, D. E. (2003). *Teaching young children in violent times: Building a peaceable classroom*. Cambridge, MA: Educators for Social Responsibility.

Levin, D. E., & Kilbourne, J. (2008). *So sexy, so soon*. New York, NY: Ballantine.

Linn, S. (2004). *Consuming kids*: The hostile takeover of childhood. New York, NY: New Press.

Linn, S. (2008). *The case for make believe: Saving play in a commercialized world*. New York, NY: The New Press.

Louv, R. (2006). *Last child in the woods*. Chapel Hill, NC: Algonquin Books.

Paige, N. C. (2008). *Taking back childhood*. New York, NY: Hudson Street Press.

Useful Websites

Alliance for Childhood: allianceforchildhood.org
Campaign for a Commercial-Free Childhood: commercialfreechildhood.org
Defending the Early Years: deyproject.org
Rethinking Schools: rethinkingschools.org
TRUCE Teachers Resisting Unhealthy Children's Entertainment: truceteachers.org

CHAPTER 5

The Struggle for Justice
U.S. History Through the Eyes of African Americans

Jenerra Williams

There are words like *Freedom*
Sweet and wonderful to say.
On my heart-strings freedom sings
All day every day.

There are words like *Liberty*
That almost make me cry.
If you had known what I knew
You would know why.

—Langston Hughes, "Refugee in America"

I read the poem aloud as the faces of 22 young students were fixed on me, these 2nd- and 3rd-graders listening intently—some faces blank with unknowing, some curious with the desire to know, some full of expression at the surprise in knowing what the poem meant. As I read the poem, emotion filled me. Langston Hughes is one of my favorite poets. Not just because I too am a poet, or because he was, like I am, African American, but because his words have the ability to speak truth and reveal the honest shortcomings of humankind while simultaneously leaving behind an intentional pathway to hope. When I think about teaching our "Struggle for Justice" theme through the lens of the African American experience, this too is my intention: Speak truth, birth hope. A thematic unit is the perfect vehicle for this. It allows teachers and students to go deeper, to observe closer, to think longer. It allows more time for thoughtful conversations that evoke questions and illuminate the insights of both children and adults. It allows the flexibility to reach a wide variety of learners. And it allows me to work closely with my colleagues to create curriculum that will engage students, sustain learning, and create powerful thinkers.

Twelve years ago I would find myself in the hallway of the Mission Hill School, sitting on a stage and reading to a 1st-grader as a part of my pre-practicum requirements. I was attending Northeastern University, obtaining my master's in education. At some point during my last year, a lightbulb flashed above my head, or as I like to believe, God revealed his calling and I decided to become a teacher. I chose Mission Hill for my practicum site knowing absolutely nothing about progressive education, democratic governance, and so on. All I knew was that I had a passion for teaching children and was committed to teaching children of color.

After that pre-practicum experience, I knew without a doubt that *this* was the kind of teaching I wanted to do and asked to be placed there for my full-time practicum experience. As things would go, a 2nd/3rd-grade position became available for the next fall. Though I did not yet see it in myself, my colleagues saw potential in me and took a chance on a brand-new teacher. Fourteen years later, I am still as passionate as on day one, less afraid, wiser, more confident, and just as passionate—maybe even more.

What I didn't know about Mission Hill in year one, I certainly know now. The philosophies and understandings that the school's foundation is built on are now a part of my teaching and learning. The five habits of mind is one of those foundations. These habits (Evidence, Connections, Viewpoint, Conjecture, Relevance) are the essential drivers of all our teaching and learning at Mission Hill. As educators we believe that these are essential habits to develop in becoming a true critical thinker and productive member of a democratic society. As articulated in our mission statement:

> Such habits of mind, and such competence, are sustained by our enthusiasms, as well as our love for others and our respect for ourselves, and our willingness to persevere, deal with frustration and develop reliable habits of work. Our mission is to create a community in which our children and their families can best maintain and nurture such democratic habits. (Mission Hill School, 2014)

We incorporate them into every aspect of the school community. Whether we are looking at the budget (what if we decided to put more money into professional development?), meeting with a family (here is the evidence that your child is a more independent learner), or planning a lesson (how will children this age understand segregation?), these habits are both inherently there and specifically placed in our work. Teachers look for these habits in each other's curriculum, and specifically the schoolwide themes. When they are present, we highlight them and help each other think about how to present them and discuss them with children.

Viewpoint is one of those habits. As a school we believe it is important for children to learn to step into the shoes of another, to be able to see another's viewpoint, whether we agree with it or not. We should be able to compare it with our own and have the tools to think critically about that comparison. We feel it is important to foster empathy for others by walking in their shoes. This empathy is then practiced in the classroom, schoolwide, and hopefully beyond. Viewpoint is a big part of how we resolve conflict and build community schoolwide. It was also a large part of my "Struggle for Justice" curriculum.

"Struggle for Justice: The African American Experience" is the school-wide theme I feel most connected to and one that I am excited about every time it comes up in our 4-year thematic cycle. From questions I posed, to projects we worked on, to understandings we left with, I will share what we learned from our study and from each other. I will also describe different aspects of how I collaborated with my colleagues to make this a successful theme.

Here are the big questions my students and I were thinking about and kept coming back to:

Essential understandings

There is power in numbers and solidarity.
It takes courage to get justice / create change.
Art can tell the story of people's lives and experiences.

Essential questions

How can hearing or knowing someone's story change your
    viewpoint?
What rights do you fight for?
When is justice served?
When does being different affect equality?

The objective of this curriculum was to use black-and-white civil rights photographs, songs, and poems to help students learn about and discuss the words *equality, courage,* and *justice*. In that process students thought about and answered the essential questions of the unit. They discussed what it felt like to be treated differently, to live in a democracy but not have a voice, and the power of a story to change someone's viewpoint.

We began the theme by examining one specific picture (shown here), a poem ("Refugee in America"), and a song ("Oh Freedom"). After we looked at or listened to these works, I asked, "What story do these three things tell? What can we learn from the stories of other people? How was/ can your viewpoint about something be changed?" This was the catalyst for several weeks of looking closely at songs, photographs, and poems by

Selma, Alabama, 1965: Led by Martin Luther King Jr., a group of civil rights demonstrators march from Selma to Montgomery to fight for black suffrage.

Photo by Bruce Davidson. Image courtesy of Magnum Photos.

African Americans and including African Americans as we developed our understanding of the civil rights movement and how it connects to us individually and as a group.

After gaining background information on African Americans in the United States, what rights they were fighting for and why, children began to dive deeper into making meaning by looking at artistic representations of the struggle. Employing the umbrella words *equality, courage*, and *justice*, we paired a black-and-white photograph from the civil rights era with a song or poem written by an African American that connected to that time period. The topics were

- Equality—The right to education and to vote
- Equality—The right to be in public places, attend events, use public facilities, or join the military, among others
- Courage—*Brown v. Board of Education*, Little Rock 9, Ruby Bridges, Freedom Summer
- Courage—March from Selma to Montgomery, March on Washington, sit-ins, boycotts
- Justice—*Brown v. Board of Education*, Voting Rights Act
- Justice—Civil Rights Act

Using the Visual Thinking Strategy (from our work with the Gardner Museum in Boston), we dissected each photograph and the written pieces that accompanied them. From there, students were asked to create similar pieces from their viewpoint, using their new understanding and their personal experience and beliefs about each topic. These pieces, along with our classroom discussions, would serve as assessment pieces.

For example, after talking about different freedom songs used during the civil rights movement like "Oh Freedom" and "Ain't Gonna Let Nobody Turn Me Around," students were given the challenge to create their own freedom song. Using some familiar tunes, they wrote original freedom songs that were recorded and compiled. Likewise, after looking at Langston Hughes's "Refugee in America" poem (Hughes, 1990, p. 290) they drafted their own poems in the same style. Here is an example:

Freedom / Justice by R. Harter

There are words like freedom
So sweet and wonderful to me.
What the world was back then
It was so unfair to me.

There are words like Justice
That's what's happening to *you* now
But what's happening to me now,
It's nowhere to be found.
It's nowhere to be found.

This work went on for about 9 weeks and culminated in a Civil Rights Arts Share, during which students were able to showcase the projects they undertook. Among the projects were a class-made book of poems and reading of poems, songs they wrote and recorded, class-made quilts inspired by those used in the Underground Railroad), and a small-scale plantation model.

For many reasons, this curriculum lent itself well to differentiation of instruction. In that regard, I will outline three of its main advantages: multiple entry points, multiple modalities of learning, and multiple forms of assessment.

First, children were given access to the curriculum through different means—photographs, songs, poetry, and stories. Presenting these various avenues of entry during every new stage of learning allowed students to connect with the material in their own way. For students who felt intimidated by poetry or other literature, there were music and photographs they could connect to. Likewise, for those who loved poetry and writing, these were their entry points. Students were able to approach the curriculum from an angle they were already interested in, using a vehicle that they were naturally attracted to and in which they were even experts.

Second, this curriculum accommodated the various learning styles of my students. For visual learners there were the photographs. For audible learners, there were the songs. For hands-on/kinesthetic learners, we had projects and the re-staging of old photographs. Also, the Visual Thinking Strategies method of looking at the pictures was a nonthreatening tool to encourage the sharing of thoughts. It emphasizes that there are no wrong answers and encourages opinions and connections. Children are saying literally what they see. For example, "I see a man standing behind a fence." This both encourages the use of familiar vocabulary and gives a chance for new vocabulary to be introduced at the same time.

Third, I was able to use different forms of assessment. There were written assessments (song lyrics, poetry), students' individual/group projects (Abraham Lincoln research with re-created diary), the Visual Thinking Strategy process, class discussions, and the performance of the students' poetry and songs. The different avenues allowed children to show what they had learned in ways that suited them. For example, one of the essential understandings was it takes courage to get justice and to make change. When students wrote poems, I looked for thoughts and words in their work that showed their understanding of the word *courage* and a civil rights leader connected to that word. The following poem met these criteria:

The Civil Rights

The North Star fills the night sky.
Going to freedom is very important to slaves.
Sometimes snakes guard the way to freedom.
Harriet Tubman would show the way to freedom.
Slaves have the right to go to freedom.

Another example is that I also looked for evidence in their work that spoke to the elements of change and justice, as the following poem did:

WE

Together we stand and our foundation is strong. We are strong together and together we stand. We will not give up in our fight for freedom. We will not give up. Two is better than one and when our fight is over we will stand and be strong. Our freedom is like a bridge. When we cross it we are free!

Rarely, if ever, does a curriculum roll out perfectly. Looking back, I note that there were a few things I would have done differently. The use of the black-and-white photos made for a wonderful tool; however, I was the person who had chosen them all. Next time, I would give students the chance to look through a large amount of those photos and choose which one or ones they wanted to learn about instead of my picking them all. I might also have students create a piece of art that speaks to a particular struggle in their life, community, or school and connect it to something they learned about the civil rights movement. Further, I would work harder to find grown-ups connected to the movement to come in and share with us as primary sources.

Although this curriculum may not be able to be used elsewhere in its entirety or in the same way that my students and I experienced it, there are parts of it that can be used in almost any classroom or other learning environment. It elicits deeper thinking beyond just what you "see" and encourages a sincere dialogue between teacher and students in which connections are being made, viewpoints taken, and conjectures offered. The practice of looking closely at the items and objectively stating what you notice and what you think is happening can be carried out equally by using civil rights photographs, scientific diagrams, the steps of a complicated equation, or the words of a historical speech. Pairing this short activity with the right questions to push students' thinking is always fruitful.

When we began our study, the whole school was engaged. Topics concerning civil rights and slavery; questions of race, equity, and fairness; celebrations of contributions by African Americans; and much more were alive in the school. Displays outside classrooms, Friday Share songs, and evidence of projects in progress were only a few of the many ways in which outsiders could witness what we were all learning about. To stay in tune with what was happening, we as teachers and staff had ongoing conversations about the theme. These took shape in several forms.

One was age pair meetings. Age pairs (two, or more, teachers working with the same grade level) met weekly to check in about how the curriculum was playing out in our classrooms. We would share student work, present dilemmas that had arisen during the course of a project, and discuss what questions to ask to move children's thinking forward. For example, at one meeting I needed help thinking about what questions to ask in connection with a photograph I was going to share with the children. My dilemma was that I had shown them a photo depicting a boycott previously, this one also was on that subject, and I didn't want to ask the same questions again. Through the process of looking at the photographs together and examining my essential questions and goals, the team helped me draft three different questions that really got at the essence of why I had chosen this new photograph.

We also met in "house meetings." House meetings were composed of teachers and cross-grade-level and other nonclassroom staff (e.g., the speech therapist or librarian) who, like age pairs, met once a week. In the house meeting teachers have a chance to hear a variety of viewpoints on our teaching and curriculum. It was during a house meeting that one of the most engaging and fruitful projects of my curriculum was initiated. I had been describing my activities with my students when one of my colleagues suggested that in addition to my having students write freedom songs, we should find a way to record them—with music. I immediately loved the idea and we began brainstorming as a house how this could happen. We came up with three ideas that worked. There were three musicians whom I realized I had access to in the school community, and two were in my classroom! I had two students in my classroom who had a parent who was a musician, one a guitar player and the other a pianist. There was also an intern in the school at the time who played guitar. I asked them all to donate time to help my budding musicians create and record music to go along with the lyrics they had written. They all agreed and by the end we had not only a *Songs of Freedom* songbook but also a CD with all their songs on it. We shared our CD with the whole school. That happened only because of the collaborative work I had done with my colleagues.

Thematic units allow time for children to be exposed to new ideas in a way that engenders questions and fosters connections. Depth over breadth—it is a notion that is sorely missing from most school curricula and one that I cherish, promote, and advocate for all children. Simply knowing that Rosa Parks sat at the front of the bus or that Martin Luther King Jr. gave his "I Have a Dream" speech alone may not make you want to fight for social justice. However, reading King's speech and talking about connections, making conjectures, taking into account his and his opponents' viewpoints, and finding evidence of why the speech was so effective at the time it was made and then writing your own speech and giving it will definitely encourage you to think deeply about King's speech. Creating and thinking about thematic units help to answer a question that is not often asked in conversations these days about the state of education: What is the *purpose* of education—is it to fill our minds with facts that we store up and pull out randomly when needed or is it to learn those facts and use them to build something better for ourselves, our community, and beyond? I would argue that it is the latter and that if we want our children to build something better, we need to consider how we are teaching them to do that and to have the courage to do it. We also need to remember that teaching should never be done in a vacuum. Not only should collaborative teaching be done, it should be demanded by educators and valued as the indispensable teaching tool that it is.

REFERENCES

Hughes, L. (1990). *Selected poems of Langston Hughes*. New York, NY: Knopf Doubleday.

Mission Hill School. (2014). Our mission. Retrieved from www.missionhillschool.org/mhs/Mission.html

CHAPTER 6

Astronomical Inquiries

Matthew Knoester

"Do planets reflect light from the sun like the moon does?" "Why don't planets in the sky look like the moon?" "What is a satellite?" "Did a meteor hit the Earth and cause the dinosaurs to die?"

    These are some of the questions kids in the Husky class asked during our brainstorm about astronomy and space this week. Excitement is in the air as students wonder about and debate these questions. Huskies are also choosing a particular astronomer (either ancient or more modern) to become an "expert" about and to learn about the technology and information used during his or her lifetime. We've gathered lots of materials for our model-building of the universe. One way to experience astronomy firsthand is with our moon sightings. Without the need for a telescope or any other assistance, Huskies are on the watch for the moon and keeping a moon journal. Day and night! Already several kids have written a page in their moon journal and drawn how it looked. Can we predict where we will see it next? Will it look different from the last time we saw it? These are questions we'll talk about throughout the spring during our morning meetings—and it's the new part of our homework each week until the end of the school year!

This was a column I wrote for the weekly *Mission Hill School News* just as I was beginning to lead a study of astronomy with my class of 9- to 11-year-olds within the schoolwide theme of "Physical Science." ("Huskies" refers to our class's nickname.) Each week, this 250-word column allowed me to share with parents and families—throughout the school—how and why we explored physical science and astronomy together. In this chapter, I describe in more depth my thinking about this 3-month theme. I draw on my experience as a teacher at Mission Hill School and on a research project I conducted about the school, involving interviews with 63 people intimately connected with the school and including a survey of all its graduates. (This was later published as a book, *Democratic Education in Practice: Inside the Mission Hill School* [Knoester, 2012].)

STRUGGLING WITH PIAGET AND DUCKWORTH'S NOTION OF (DIS)EQUILIBRIUM

Before I describe how I developed and led this thematic unit, allow me to mention the influence of a particular person on my scientific and educational thinking and on that of many others at Mission Hill School. Eleanor Duckworth is a professor emerita at Harvard University and was a colleague of Jean Piaget in Geneva and strongly influenced by his ideas about human learning and development. Duckworth is also an old friend of Deborah Meier and one of the first people who encouraged Meier to open the Mission Hill School. Duckworth has led courses at the school for both Harvard students and Mission Hill staff on several occasions, and I was lucky enough to take two of those classes at Mission Hill as well as three additional courses with her at Harvard when I was a student there.

One of the key points that Duckworth pushes her students to think about is how students need to struggle with ideas in order to significantly shift current understandings. She builds on the work of Piaget, who transferred his knowledge of equilibrium in biology to his thinking about the human mind: People have a particular schema, or set of understandings, and in order to learn new concepts, either understandings must be added on to one's current schema or the schema must be significantly disrupted and a new schema must be constructed to accommodate the new understandings. Duckworth is well known in the education world for creating tasks for adults and children that are likely to disrupt their current schema and to encourage imaginative new thinking to solve problems. This is generally how she used our time together in the courses in which I was fortunate to take part, and she offers dozens of examples of such tasks in her book *The Having of Wonderful Ideas* (Duckworth, 1996). Throughout, she emphasized that different people can have (are likely to have) different understandings of the "same phenomena" and that these differences need to be respected. She writes, "I have found a vast array of ways that people come to their understanding—a vast array of perfectly adequate ways" (p. xi).

As I planned for the unit that I describe in this chapter, and in fact for all the units that I have planned, I have thought about these words and ideas. How can I both provide enriching information and experiences for children and allow for students' different ways of knowing? How can I challenge students to create more adequate understandings of the world around them while also recognizing that their current understandings do not amount to a "deficit" of knowledge but that it is with their current knowledge that new knowledge can be constructed? And how do I make space for the "emergent curriculum" that might arise from students' interests and curiosities about the world around them?

TRANSITIONING FROM GREECE TO ASTRONOMY

Before deciding how I would focus my class's explorations within "Physical Science," I consulted extensively with colleagues about various options and ideas for activities and resources within these explorations during one of our staff retreats (retreats take place three times a year). One concern that I had, for example—and a concern shared by colleagues—in choosing to study astronomy was whether I could find a balance between teaching particular facts about astronomy and children's discovering and playing with ideas on their own within this broad field. In other words, how could I draw upon the ideas of Duckworth and Piaget to create spaces for exploration? I am not sure that I struck a perfect balance, but the unit included firsthand explorations, as well as reading aloud particular stories and articles, hearing speakers, and viewing presentations about historical discoveries related to astronomy.

The schoolwide unit immediately preceding this one was an exploration of ancient Greece, during which students in my class had created beautifully bound books of original creation myths that featured various Greek gods and goddesses. We learned about Homer's epics and we held a symposium—and read parts of Plato's *Symposium*—with Greek food and music and partook in a philosophical debate on the meaning of the word *courage*, in which students stood up and made speeches about the courage they saw in their classmates. After deep immersion in meaningful explorations of ancient cultures such as this it is sometimes difficult to make a transition to an entirely new topic.

So I decided to begin our "Physical Science" unit by building on this knowledge and inquiring into remnants of ancient Greece in our current lives, focusing on the names of the days of the week and months of the year, many of which were named after Greek (or Roman) gods. I encouraged students to practice the habit of mind of Connections (asking, "How is what I am learning connected to what I already know?") to notice how our daily use of these words were connected to ancient beliefs, and the habit of Relevance (asking, "Why does it matter?") by asking what they knew about how days of the week and months of the year were determined and what this might have to do with the movements of our planet (and that many of the planets in our solar system are named after Greek or Roman gods as well). I read aloud stories to the students about ancient astronomers such as Pythagoras, Hipparchus, and Aristotle. As a group, we tried to understand how these men understood the composition of the universe and various celestial bodies' movements and how these understandings might compare with current understandings. Then, drawing on the habit of mind of Evidence (asking, "How do you know what you know?") I challenged students to explain why some theories of our planet and the solar system might be correct and others not. And if ancient astronomers were known as "brilliant," how is it that their theories could be so different from current understandings? This, of course, drew on the habit of mind of Perspective (asking, "From whose perspective am I looking?") and the contrasting knowledge and experiences people in ancient times might have had as compared with those in modern times. These discussions also drew on the habit of mind of Conjecture (asking, "How could things have been different?"), requiring students to imagine a different world and also how things could have been different had particular discoveries not been made.

Another reason why I chose this subtheme within "Physical Science" is because of my own interest in the topic. One of the great benefits of broad thematic units is that teachers can bring their own interests and knowledge to their students, which may allow students to see why this area is interesting, important, or relevant to their own lives. Although I am not formally trained as an astronomer (beyond one class in college), I do have a long-standing interest in this area, have owned a telescope for many years, and have wonderful memories of visiting observatories and planetariums throughout my life. And I am forever fascinated by the history of thinking in these areas. It is possible to know a great deal about how scientific thinking developed over the past 3,000 years by learning more about the astronomers who contributed to this conversation. There are facts about some of these astronomers that continually surprise me. For example, did you know that the ancient astronomer Hipparchus, who lived about 190–120 BC, is considered the founder of trigonometry? That is a long time ago, and I struggled with learning trigonometry in my lifetime. He also is known to have invented highly complex astrolabes that can be used to predict the movements of the sun and moon, including eclipses of the sun (none of his astrolabes survive). Did you know that Aristarchus, who lived even before Hipparchus, theorized that the earth revolved around the sun? Most scientific historians claim that Copernicus was the first person to do this, in 1543, but he was not. Aristarchus knew this nearly 2,000 years before Copernicus, but he was eventually overshadowed by the enormous influence of Ptolemy and Aristotle (and the Catholic Church). It is interesting to compare contrasting views of these matters held by people who were considered so important in their day.

One of the great tragedies of the ancient world was the burning(s) of the enormous library in Alexandria, Egypt (the exact date or dates of the fire or multiple fires is or are disputed but generally associated with the Roman conquest of Egypt). This library was known to house the only copies of many important scientific discoveries of the ancient world. Imagine what we would have known if this knowledge had been preserved.

CONFRONTING INTUITION AND COMMON UNDERSTANDINGS WITH EXPERIMENTS IN PHYSICAL SCIENCE

One feature of studying space and planets for us was looking at how atmospheres in different locations (i.e., planets) and air changes, depending on various conditions. As part of this exploration I led the students in a study of Earth's atmosphere, and especially one aspect of it: the fact that the air surrounding our planet has distinct properties. One of these properties is that it takes up space. Drawing from websites and books, such as Tom Robinson's *The Everything Kids' Science Experiments Book* (2001), I led demonstrations and experiments that revealed a few counterintuitive aspects of air.

Most people (myself included) generally assume that air is "nothing." But it's possible to show quite dramatically that air is something—it is matter. One way of showing this is by taking an empty plastic bottle and placing a funnel in the bottle's spout. Then, use Silly Putty or clay to seal the space between the bottle's mouth and the funnel. Next, pour water into the funnel. What happens? The water does not enter the bottle. Before passing around bottles and clay to students to try this out, I asked students what would happen to the water and most said it would enter the bottle. What we discovered was that water wasn't entering the bottle (unless the space around the funnel was not completely plugged). "You plugged it," one student said to another. "No, I didn't," another replied, trying to tilt the bottle to show the hole in the funnel. "There's an invisible force in there," another student suggested. When students had experimented with the materials for several minutes we gathered together again and I began to explain that air takes up space, so if air is not able to escape from the bottle, water cannot enter into it! This phrase, *air takes up space*, became a refrain, so as I made more demonstrations, and we experimented with more materials, students began to predict the answer.

Next, we built a very sensitive balance by tying a string to the middle of a yardstick and taping balloons to either end of the stick. The stick would tilt to the right or the left very easily. On one side was a balloon that was filled with air; on another, a balloon without air. Which weighed more? The yardstick balance showed the one with air weighed more! Of course, there were all kinds of things I could have done to "rig" the stick, according to some students, such as using more tape on one side than the other, so I don't think I persuaded too many students with that one.

This area of exploration also involved reading about and experimenting with the concept of "lift." Reading aloud books such as Terry Jennings's *How Things Work: Planes, Gliders, and Helicopters, and Other Flying Machines*

(1993), we were able to have discussions about why heavy objects like airplanes can fly. Students also made and flew many kinds of paper airplanes and experimented with various designs, and I was able to show the video that was taken of me parachuting out of an airplane and surviving (I spent the extra money to hire a videographer with a camera mounted on his helmet to jump with me)—none of which could have taken place if air didn't take up space. In these explorations I was able to combine aspects of students moving from one understanding to a new one through their own trial and error with paper airplanes, for example, and just through being confronted with ideas that challenged previous understandings.

Here is a column that I wrote in the *Mission Hill School News* during this exploration:

> Our new unit on astronomy has officially blasted off (forgive the pun). On Monday the moon was located directly out of our classroom window at 10:00 a.m. and gave us a perfect opportunity to look at it through our telescope. "It's huge!" Abdirahman said after looking through the lens. "Why is it backwards?" Emily asked. She was right. Since our telescope uses a mirror the objects in view appear backwards or upside down.
>
> We've been talking about the scientific method. First, scientists state a hypothesis. Next, they design an experiment that tests the theory. Finally, they collect data and analyze the results to make a conclusion and perhaps form a new hypothesis. As we have been making observations of the moon, several students have made hypotheses as to how it moves in relation to the Earth. Students should be writing their hypotheses in their moon journals.
>
> Another finding of science is that the air around us takes up space. We demonstrated this last week using a bottle with tissue paper stuffed inside. We placed the capless bottle upside down into a bucket of water. As long as we didn't allow any air to escape from the bottle the tissues stayed dry. Is it magic? No, it's science—and evidence that air takes up space!

STARGAZING

As suggested above, this unit also involved stargazing. I read aloud many books and articles focusing on topics relating to celestial bodies and space, such as Ellen Hansbrouk and Scott McDougall's *Planets* (2001) and Laura Evert's *Planets, Moons, and Stars* (2003), and students chose books from various libraries (such as the local public library and our school library) and articles from the Internet (they especially loved looking at photos on the NASA website) to read during quiet reading time in class—I also amassed a large number of these books and articles as the unit was getting under way. We observed the movements of the moon through a telescope in the classroom and took the telescope outside, and I organized a family trip to the telescopes at Boston University one evening, where we could directly see the rings around Saturn, the spot on Jupiter, and moons around both these planets. The whole class also had the opportunity to visit the infrared telescope control center at the Harvard-Smithsonian astrophysics lab in Cambridge. We had a guest speaker come in, John McSweeney, who was the former director of the Harvard-Smithsonian astrophysics lab, and students took detailed notes in their journals about their observations of the moon, followed by debates about where they predicted they would see the moon next and in what phase, again drawing on the habit of mind of Evidence.

Stargazing, or perhaps more accurately, *moongazing*, was one key way that I was able to incorporate the ideas of Eleanor Duckworth in this unit. Duckworth is well known for leading adults in an inquiry of the movements of the moon (and the earth in relation to it). In one of my courses with her, for example, Duckworth asked each of her students to keep track of the moon and to make notes of their observations and questions in a "moon journal." During class time, her adult students would share their observations and queries and make predictions about where they might see the moon next. The moon is often a central figure in children's storybooks, in nursery rhymes, and in children's drawings of the night sky. And yet it is amazing how little knowledge most adults have about the movements of the moon (and our movements in relation to it). Try this thought experiment: Do you know where the moon can be seen right now—in which direction and how far above the horizon? Do you know where it might be seen where you are tonight at about 10 p.m.? My guess is that, unless you are an avid watcher of the moon, you probably do not. I don't! And so it is a lot of fun to start keeping track of moon observations and to develop theories about what is happening with the moon. This is also a fun activity for children. They already know quite a bit about the moon, from the sources I mentioned above. But what about its movements? What can we learn from close observations of its craters and shadows through a telescope? And why does the same side of the moon always face the Earth? New theories can be generated about these topics as well. It was often hard to get a good glimpse of the moon during the school day, but we took the telescope outside on many occasions and gazed up at what we saw.

Another experiment that we tried in class (suggested by Deborah Meier) was to try to explain, using only the tools we had available, that the earth was not flat but round. It is very difficult to do this without referring to some form of modern technology, such as photographs taken by astronauts in space or our experience of flying in airplanes. We also borrowed from Duckworth's book the idea of trying to prove to one another a concept that is taken for granted by many adults as well as children: "What is north?" It might seem obvious at first, but what if you are standing at the North Pole? What if the magnetic poles of the earth shift (as they do slowly, and then quickly, periodically). Thinking through scientific principles and concepts and questioning one's given assumptions require students to draw on the habits of mind to think critically. It also sometimes means that we must all learn to live with ambiguity and mystery about many large questions about our existence.

At one point we were able to take a class trip to the planetarium at the Boston Museum of Science, which was a new experience for many students. Although this experience is more like a presentation, such as a film, and was perhaps less likely to cause children to generate new ideas or thought processes about how planets, moons, and stars move and other concepts related to astronomy, the unique experience of being surrounded by visuals under a dark dome could provide the feeling of immersion within the thematic unit we were thinking about every day.

CULMINATION

The culmination of the unit was a long-term project that involved each student in the class choosing a famous astronomer on whom to become an expert. Some students chose ancient astronomers, such as Pythagoras, Aristarchus, and Aristotle, and others chose more recent astronomers, such as Copernicus, Galileo, and most recent of all, Stephen Hawking. Each student chose a different astronomer. The students' task was to understand their astronomer's view of the universe; to summarize it in a two-page paper, several drafts of which were written to correct for coherence, grammar, style, and conventions; and to make a model of the solar system according to their astronomer. I chose to ask students to create models of the solar system because this was one way to compare astronomers' views and to demonstrate the history of knowledge in this area. These models revealed fascinating facts. For instance, there was an influential Pythagorean mathematician and scientist named Philolaus who held a quite interesting view of the universe. The ancient anthologist Stobaeus described it in this way:

> There is fire in the middle at the centre . . . and again more fire at the highest point and surrounding everything. By nature the middle is first, and around it dance ten divine bodies—the sky, the planets, then the sun, next the moon, next the earth, next the counterearth, and after all of them the fire of the hearth which holds position at the centre. The highest part of the surrounding, where the elements are found in their purity, he calls Olympus; the re-

gions beneath the orbit of Olympus, where are the five planets with the sun and the moon, he calls the world; the part under them, being beneath the moon and around the earth, in which are found generation and change, he calls the sky. (Barnes, 2001, p. 179)

The student who chose Philolaus seemed to have a lot of fun creating a model of the solar system according to this understanding. Students were then asked to create an aesthetically appealing posterboard with information and pictures about their astronomer placed next to their model of the solar system, models that were constructed from a range of materials, including Styrofoam balls, bent wire, paint, and different-colored clay, all provided by the school.

Toward the end of the astronomy theme our class organized a "space museum" to present our work. We set several dates that might make it convenient for parents and others in the school to attend. When the museum was open, visitors could walk through our darkened classroom and see the posterboards and solar system models that the students had created. Eerie space music played in the background and students wore black, to focus attention on their creations. The students each had a flashlight and they stood by their creations, shining the light on them. They explained to each passerby what they had created and answered any questions a student or adult visitor might have. The posterboards and models were placed in chronological order, so it was possible to see the development of scientific ideas having to do with the solar system over time. I heard many positive comments from visitors to the museum about how well informed the students seemed to be about astronomy and about their chosen astronomer in particular.

INFLUENCE OF RON BERGER AND TEACHING WITH CRITIQUE

One of the unique aspects of the Mission Hill School approach to curriculum is the significant attention given to providing powerful learning opportunities for all students with their myriad abilities and interests while not tracking students into rigid ability groups. All students in my classroom completed a beautiful posterboard and model of their astronomer's view of the solar system, but some required supports that others might not have needed. When planning interdisciplinary culminating projects toward the end of thematic units that involve many components, often only some of the components are required for all students and others are extensions for students who may rise to a particular challenge. In my classroom, for example, some students included many more facts and research on their posterboard than the required minimum. Still, the projects of all students were aesthetically pleasing, artistic, presentable, and the result of hard work.

The class time planned for these culminating projects generally involved a teaching technique called critique and the use of multiple drafts, such as that described by Ron Berger (2003; Knoester, 2004). The entire staff at Mission Hill read Berger's book *An Ethic of Excellence: Building a culture of craftsmanship with students,* and we were fortunate to have a professional development workshop led by him at one point. He brought a large pile of his students' work, which was very impressive, and persuaded us to lead students through a series of drafts of culminating projects in order to make the work impressive to the student him- or herself, and also to the entire community.

In such a process, drafts of student work are subject to a critique involving students and a teacher, a critique that is carefully monitored to include compliments and kind suggestions for improvement for the next draft. This process could be around a student's piece of writing, scale model, drawing, or almost any other task or product that might be improved with another draft. In the astronomy theme, students undertook critiques of both their two-page research paper and of their model of the solar system. This teaching technique is also not easy, as a culture of kindness and noncompetitiveness is required for all students to feel safe while their work is being critiqued. The development of this classroom culture must be part of an ongoing curriculum throughout the year. This technique allows students of all abilities to succeed, if the culture of the classroom is one of mutual support, rather than competition. Further, teachers can plan projects with multiple levels of achievement, allowing some students to complete a larger number of tasks, or to complete the tasks while building on their strengths, which might be a particular knowledge set or a form of intelligence—such as a more visual, musical, verbal, or written approach. In the astronomy unit, some students completed longer research papers, more than one model, and other variations on the presentation.

Mission Hill staff members believe that what is motivating for children is the meaning that they are making in their explorations, the communities of which they are a part, and the performances or public successes that allow them to develop a strong public academic identity.

Students heard well-deserved compliments about their work from nearly every visitor who came to the culminating space museum. Setting students up for this public acknowledgment was a key intention of this unit. Adults asked challenging questions and the presenting students almost always rose to the occasion, further impressing their audience. In addition, this museum allowed the rest of the students in the school to enhance their understanding of physical science and astronomy through our research and presentations.

Another way in which I think and plan for differentiation in my classroom is through the more general allowance of choices in the classroom, including giving students a choice of the order of tasks they will complete during a given class period, week, or even longer period of time. Toward the end of the chapter I describe how the class schedule looks in more detail. Many of the projects and tasks I ask of students require students to plan their time, a skill or mindset that Mission Hill School teachers believe is an important life skill. This way of teaching is called the "integrated day" at Mission Hill.

This form of teaching requires more time spent in preparation than simply teaching in a one-size-fits-all manner from a textbook. But Mission Hill School teachers believe the extra preparation is essential. For example, when teaching within an interdisciplinary thematic unit, it is often difficult to find reading material that is the precise reading level necessary for the students in each class. This means I am often finding reading material that is interesting and informative for my students and relevant to the theme but sometimes rewriting it so it is at the appropriate reading level, or creating math or science inquiries that are based on the problems scientists may use in a particular physical or natural science theme, but adjusting for the skill level of students. This is one of the challenges in creating responsive and challenging curricula for a wide range of learners.

A significant number of learning goals were reached by the end of this unit. As indicated above, the habits of mind for critical thinking were practiced throughout. When inquiring into the etymology of words or the historical record of scientific discovery, debating the merits of contrasting astronomical theories, and imagining where they might see the moon next, students put the habits of mind to work. Then the museum set students up for authentic compliments on their work by adults and peers alike, which allowed students to strengthen their identity development as serious and engaged students. Detailed note taking and writing was involved in various aspects of this thematic unit, and reading for information and a significant amount of mathematical reasoning were involved in discussing the size and distance of various celestial bodies, building models, and learning about how astronomy could be used for ship navigation using the Pythagorean theorem, among other tasks.

Although science units do not often focus on issues of social justice, as compared with social studies units, within this unit we were able to discuss issues surrounding the persecution of Galileo and other scientists who dared question religious orthodoxy, as well as issues of gender discrimination, such as the fact that educational opportunities were often not available to girls but there were nevertheless outstanding women astronomers in history, such as the 4th-century Greek scholar Hypatia. Similarly, racial discrimination prevented many men and women of African descent from obtaining an education and yet outstanding black astronomers such as Benjamin Banneker have made significant discoveries and contributions. Both Hypatia and Banneker were chosen by students to be worthy of in-depth study and presented in our museum.

TYPICAL SCHEDULE

Here is how a typical class schedule might look in my classroom (thematic work can happen during each period, but in different form):

8:30 Morning activities. Since students trickle in, they take part in assigned rotational groups that are occupied with quiet independent activities, such as quiet reading, math puzzles, math or reading computer activities, or one-on-one work with me.

9:15 Morning meeting. During this time two student leaders will lead the class, going over the schedule for the day, taking attendance, asking students to volunteer to share news about their personal or family lives, and then supervising a group activity such as a game or solving a set of riddles or a mystery.

9:45 Math. During this time the 4th- and 5th-graders divide to work on their grade-level math with their math instructors and I will teach the 5th-grade group using the TERC *Investigations* curriculum (investigations.terc.edu), supplemented with math from Marilyn Burns and other resources.

10:45 Literacy. During this time my 4th- and 5th-graders will return to their homeroom and work on literacy—focusing either on reading or writing workshop. They may be conducting research or writing a draft of a research paper or, especially toward the beginning of a thematic unit, involved with a literature circle—working with a small group of four or five students to read one book together, each assigned a role to play in discussing and analyzing the book, usually within the scope of the thematic unit.

11:30 Lunch and recess.

12:30 Specials. During this time the students will work with a PE teacher, the art teacher, or the music teacher.

1:30 Read aloud. During this time I will read a book aloud to the students. They often are drawing or doing art while I am reading aloud. The book is always providing information within the thematic unit.

2:00 Project time. During this time students sign up for one of the areas to work in. They may "drop in" to the art room to work on a project, they might be working on their solar system for the thematic unit, they might conduct research on the Internet or using books, or they might be engaged in other choices. Before we break up we talk about exactly what each student's goal is for that period of time.

2:55 Cleanup time. During this time students straighten out the room and work on their class job, which is assigned to them on a rotational basis, such as feeding the guinea pig, watering the plants, straightening up the books, or vacuuming the rug.

3:05 Closing circle. During this time we talk about what we accomplished that day and what students are particularly proud of. I also give reminders about things that need to be done in the coming days. Finally, we play or sing several songs. Usually I accompany with guitar and students pick a song from the shared song book or we conduct a "drum circle," where a student starts a rhythm and each student adds another rhythm onto it.

This is just one example of a regular schedule. Fridays are markedly different, since the entire school meets together to share our work at Friday Share. There is usually a fieldtrip to be taken approximately once a week, we often have guest speakers, and other changes in the schedule can affect how it looks from day to day. But it is possible to see in this schedule that, although there is structure and predictability, students are given quite a lot of decisionmaking and leadership opportunities in their own education and are able to immerse themselves in the thematic unit throughout many parts of the day.

TEACHING MATH AT MISSION HILL SCHOOL

Here is another column I wrote for the *Mission Hill School News* toward the middle of our astronomy unit:

As students in the Husky class continue their astronomy research and model building, some of the most fun parts of the day happen at meeting when kids discuss more and more questions. What makes astronomers think there was a Big Bang? Is the universe expanding? Will it contract after it expands? What is a black hole? How are gamma rays, X-rays, and infrared rays used to know about stars and galaxies? Some ask existential questions; is there life outside of Earth?

It is amazing how many times we refer to knowledge from ancient civilizations during our study. People have been astronomers for thousands of years. One of the habits of mind we've relied on heavily has been Connections. How did Galileo in the 17th century build on the work of the Greek astronomers Aristarchus from 300 B.C.? How did Einstein build on the work of Copernicus? This week we will look at pictures of Stonehenge in England and wonder about what Druids thought 5,000 years ago. They must have known something about astronomy and also how to erect structures out of 50-ton boulders (which they must have carried from miles away).

Throughout our exploration interesting concepts about science have arisen. What do gravity, magnetism, and inertia have to do with space? Kids in the Hawks classroom are studying laws of motion and the 5th-graders have fascinating exchanges during math class, of ideas around astronomy and the forces, including demonstrations meant to prove the theories of inertia and the power of magnetism. As one student mentioned, "It's a good thing gravity and inertia exist or our world would fling off into space!"

As mentioned above, there were a number of ways that the students and I were able to enhance our mathematical understandings during this thematic unit on physical science. Examples included reading about and examining ways sailors used the Pythagorean theorem to navigate vessels, and computing distances between planets, lengths of days and years on each planet, and trying to figure out the scale of planet sizes.

Still, there has been a feeling since the opening of the school that it was hard to provide enough mathematical experiences for students within thematic units. I wrote above that the Hawks classroom was studying gravity, inertia, and magnetism, while the Huskies were studying astronomy, but that the 5th-graders came together for math class. In the early years of the school, the staff adopted the TERC *Investigations* curriculum for the younger grades (K–5) and *Connected Mathematics Project* curriculum (connectedmath.msu.edu) for the middle school grades. We did this so that an hour of each day could be focused on the learning of math (see schedule above) which is also expected of students in each grade throughout the school district, while Mission Hill also ties in math concepts that are relevant to the thematic units under study.

The result has been less than ideal. At the beginning of this chapter I mentioned that I conducted an in-depth study of the school that involved surveying all the graduates of the school and interviewing 63 people intimately connected with the school, as either a staff member, graduate, or parent. The math program at the school was most often raised as the least popular aspect of the school or as an area of concern. Let me reiterate that the math program is the same one that has been adopted across the Boston Public Schools, and the school coordinates with the district to use the same textbooks and assessments and even uses the math coaching staff of the district to work with teachers at Mission Hill. The problem, according to those I interviewed for the project, is that the standardized tests required for all public schools, as well as internal tests used at Mission Hill, indicate that students have not passed the math tests at an acceptable rate (a higher rate than the district, but lower than the state average, and a rate that the state has deemed unacceptable). Therefore, the state has labeled the school as underperforming. Further, graduates in my interviews stated that the math component of the school seemed disconnected from the rest of what goes on at the school, and several graduates who were attending elite private high schools stated that the math they learned at Mission Hill was not rigorous enough for them to be ready for high school math. There have been many studies that suggest that standardized test results are closely connected to the socioeconomic status of children, and as a result of the tests' questionable validity (does the sample of questions really reflect the entirety of what a child knows?), lack of democratic input (what is on the test and who decides what is "proficient?"), and their effect of narrowing the curriculum (must I, as a teacher, discard what I know is compelling and meaningful curricula so students will do better on this misleading test?), I do not believe these tests should drive curriculum in schools. Yet Mission Hill School certainly feels this pressure, and this is part of why math is taught as a separate subject, rather than as an integrated part of the whole-school thematic units. Of course, this is a much larger topic than what is within the scope of this chapter. I have written much more about this subject elsewhere (Knoester, 2012), as has Deborah Meier (2002).

CONCLUSION

Another column I wrote for the *Mission Hill School News,* this one toward the end of our unit:

> It's been hard to find the moon during these cloudy weeks, but when it is found it makes a lasting impression! JoAnn described how she had been looking out for the moon for days when she finally found it. "It was so beautiful! It was not too high from the horizon, just three fists high. Less than half of it was reflecting light and it was in the west. It was pure white and clouds were drifting by."
>
> I hope students take away many things from this unit. I want them to know that scientific inquiry involves using evidence to make a case about the universe. Astronomers over thousands of years took time, instruments, careful notes, and mathematical thinking to arrive at our current understanding of the solar system with nine planets and moons orbiting most of the planets. And there are many more discoveries to be made! But most of all, I hope students take away a desire and interest to look at and wonder about the night sky. In ten years, students will see the moon and think about astronomy in the Husky classroom!

As I described throughout this chapter, Mission Hill spends a great deal of energy planning and carrying out a curriculum that is responsive to the way children are motivated and learn, as well as to the goal of preparing students to participate in a democracy and to be powerful members of their communities. I focused particularly on the experiential inquiries that have created a balance between students' tinkering, playing, and challenging their current understandings about physical science and providing stories, history, and facts about what scientists have learned over time. Students put together an impressive set of creations based on their research and creativity that I believe allowed them to strengthen their public academic identities and to create memorable work that may lead to lifelong learning about astronomy and physical science.

REFERENCES

Barnes, J. (2001). *Early Greek philosophy* (2nd ed.). New York, NY: Penguin Classics.

Berger, R. (2003). *An ethic of excellence: Building a culture of craftsmanship with students.* Portsmouth, NH: Heinemann.

Duckworth, E. (1996). *The having of wonderful ideas: And other essays on teaching and learning.* New York, NY: Teachers College Press.

Evert, L. (2003). *Planets, moons, and stars.* Take-along guides. Lanham, MD: Cooper Square.

Hansbrouk, E., & McDougall, S. (2001). *Planets.* New York, NY: Little Simon.

Jennings, T. (1993). *How things work: Planes, gliders, and helicopters and other flying machines.* London, UK: Kingfisher.

Knoester, M. (2004). Eavesdropping on Ron Berger's classroom. *Schools: Studies in Education, 1*(2), 166–170.

Knoester, M. (2012). *Democratic education in practice: Inside the Mission Hill School.* New York, NY: Teachers College Press.

Meier, D. (2002). *In schools we trust: Creating communities of learning in an era of testing and standardization.* Boston, MA: Beacon Press.

Robinson, T. (2001). *The everything kids' science experiments book: Boil ice, float water, measure gravity—challenge the world around you!* Fort Collins, CO: Adams Media.

CHAPTER 7

Art at Mission Hill School

Jeanne Rachko

I have come to believe that a great teacher is a great artist and that there are as few as any other great artists. Teaching might even be the greatest of the arts since the medium is the human mind and spirit.

—John Steinbeck

For the past 18 years I have had the pleasure of working with every staff member and student—as young as 3 and as old as 15—at the Mission Hill School. My daughter graduated from Mission Hill and has since graduated from college. My connections are long and deep with my school community and my work; this vocation has shaped who I am and am still becoming. This work—teaching—is always progressing, as I am in this daily practice. The challenges faced in education are met with determination and a passion to provide equitable and engaging experiences for our children.

I am proud to be a teacher at Mission Hill. Art is integrated into all subject areas and creativity is held in high regard. My work with students is given weight and value equal to that of other academic areas, and collaboration with colleagues is a key factor in Mission Hill's philosophy. Art is an academic endeavor that supports all avenues of learning with the scientific habits of careful observation, mathematical thinking, and the chemistry of life. The alchemy of art is a necessary ingredient in the attainment of learning. Creativity benefits us all!

Each year the school and the art room come alive with the sounds, textures, and artifacts of a place or time. Creating that atmosphere is one of the most enjoyable parts of my job. Theme work frames a common topic that branches off in many directions but has deep roots, agreed upon by all faculty. The roots are our common belief about social justice and democracy in education and the work of truth seeking. This is truly getting to the root of things, understanding patterns, connections, and the relevance of human history, which has an influence on all life forms. The shared responsibility to support this common understanding about teaching and learning creates a dynamic of a common vision and an accountability to one another as we hold each other's practice to a high standard, with the child at the center, and with the unwavering belief that all children deserve the highest quality of education and experience in this place we call school. Ultimately, designing a space, a classroom, and a school that pays close attention to light, color, sound, and smell will produce optimal learning experiences, with lasting and positive impressions that are imprinted on our memory of school.

> Vital lives are about action. You can't feel warmth unless you create it, can't feel delight until you play, can't know serendipity unless you risk.
>
> —Joan Erickson

I am constantly reminded that our oldest students crave the experiences that the youngest students have more often or naturally: finger painting, engaging in spin art, splattering paint, molding with clay and play dough, having unstructured play with texture, materials, and movement. My goal has always been to facilitate art making that is visceral and transcendent when at its best and to create an art space/classroom that supports an inherent need to make something ourselves, to learn and to teach others to make sense of the world through art and creativity.

The learning environment (art room) supports and enhances schoolwide theme work (content), process (engagement), and products (projects) throughout the school year. My work keeps me on my toes and I am always aware of the need for imagination, exploration, and innovation in the arts and in our school in general. Creativity is always at the forefront of my practice, as is supporting and encouraging discovery with materials and process. The process of art making has always been as important, if not more important, than the products used. At Mission Hill School, each and every student—not just the obviously gifted—is viewed as an artist. I strive to create new ways of seeing, feeling, and being, in order to preserve and honor the innate creative potential in every one of us, young and old, teacher and student.

The environment I create is a nonthreatening classroom that inspires art making and imagination with a healthy dose of play. The art room is a studio that can be pliable. Tables can be moved around for any given project. They can be pushed together for bigger projects or arranged for small-group or individual work. A variety of seating options and arrangements are always made available to suit every classroom, every child, and every need. I plan ahead for projects, buying materials or getting items through recycle centers.

The room is set up before a whole classroom has an art period. Materials are available at arm's reach and there is a larger table for drying or viewing finished art. Music is usually playing that may be (or not) related to the current theme. For example, Chinese bamboo flute music was often played during the "Ancient China" theme and "Rainforest Dream" by Mundo Taino—a mainstay playing throughout the school during our most recent Taino study—captured and showcased the sounds of coqui frogs, chirping birds, and pouring rain . . . sounding just like a rainforest!

> If facts are the seeds that later produce knowledge and wisdom, then the emotions and impressions of the senses are the fertile soil in which the seeds must grow.

> —Rachel Carson

FLOW, FUNCTION, FEELING

The classroom needs to have flow and function, with attention to detail, design, and the best use of space. I purchase materials that are appropriate for the art projects planned and make sure there is enough for every student (in the school). Scissors, glue, and pencils are sorted and intentionally placed in baskets or interesting tin cans and containers. Art supplies are kept on shelves that line a wall and are easily accessible for smaller children to reach. They are visually organized and sorted for use. These shelves also act as display areas for shells, gourds, rocks, branches, teacups, musical instruments, and other items. These objects are used for inspiration or for drawing or purely to look at. Magnifying glasses and small baskets for sorting a shell, rock, button, and bead collection are made available for students to observe, use, and explore. Because they know where things go, students help clean up and enjoy using aromatic cleaning sprays (lavender and lemon are two of their favorite scents). I make my own room sprays or mists with essential oils and keep them at hand to freshen the room. In this way cleaning supplies that are harsh or have harmful chemicals are not a part of the classroom environment. Instead, more natural smells stimulate the senses.

A window is open at all times for fresh air to circulate throughout the room, and overhead fluorescent lights are never used. Instead many different lamps that provide enough light along with the existing natural light from the windows provide a softer feel to the room. Plenty of elbow room for big projects is provided as well as a place for finished work or works in progress to dry or be on display. Maintaining and creating a visually organized space for learning is essential. When people are inspired by works of art, natural objects, and a wide variety of music, curiosity and wonder

Typical art room setup at Mission Hill

develop. With plenty of room to spread out and get messy and with space in which to play and wonder, my expectation in the art room is for our students to honor and respect the time given for art making, the materials we are working with, the art room (space), each other, and me. Routines, active listening, practices of sharing about process and product, and collective ownership and maintenance of the area help support consistency and care for the space. Furniture, objects, and textures (rugs, pillows, baskets, lamps, plants, shells, rocks, driftwood, etc.) are carefully chosen to create a multisensory space. A comfortable, welcoming classroom inspires and promotes healthy habits of productivity, play, and discovery. The aesthetic of the art room and the school has always been important to me. School should be a pleasant, beautiful, thriving place where we want to be, that we look forward to coming to, that we take care of, and that we show pride in.

MAKING THINGS

Learning by doing—making things with our hands—supports creative thinking, self-expression, pride, and the confidence to experiment and develop skills and craft. Discovery in learning is the entryway into acquiring information, gathering images, making connections, solving problems, and preparing a solid foundation of content knowledge. When originality, risk taking, and exploration are encouraged, there isn't room for a competitive learning environment. Everyone—every student, every adult—is considered a teacher and learner and given room to make mistakes. Sometimes these mistakes can lead to a breakthrough and act as a humble reminder that we are all human. Something exceptional might come from a mistake, or it can be an opportunity for growth. Leaving room for the unknown, letting things flow, and staying open and flexible in your thinking lets the process take over, and that is good for your soul. This outlook creates a classroom that supports the expectation that every student can participate and proceed at his or her own pace and in his or her own way, however that student's mark is made.

When something stirs curiosity in us, that need to know, to explore further, and to examine something closely means we are on the right path. It fuels a passion to learn, to taste, to touch, and to smell, and to wonder about the world. A rich curriculum with multiple resources and meaningful connections to our students, families, and community honors our work with students and their history, shows respect for the natural world, and acknowledges the past, present, and future. The art program is woven into schoolwide themes and deeply embedded in our school's philosophy. As I teach I continue to grow and explore with every theme, every child, every day. I stress that inspiration can be found in nature, in music, in movement, and in obvious places that showcase beautiful objects, but art can be ugly and disturbing as well. It can stir in us questions, judgment, or fear. As long as it makes us think, rattles us, moves us out of our comfort zone, art opens the door and helps us to grow.

> But most of all, the truth, that dangerous stuff, became beautiful and more precious.
>
> —John Steinbeck

WHOLE-CLASS ART AND "OPEN STUDIO"

My weekly schedule changes year to year as classrooms change or grow. There has always been a huge degree of flexibility in my classroom work, in a balance with function and necessary expectations. I can explain this further by saying that in an attempt to meet the needs of every classroom there is always a time grid involved. I schedule with the homeroom teacher an hour of art a week (sometimes a little more). The whole-class art schedule provides an hour of scheduled art per classroom every week. This time is designed to integrate the whole-school theme with art. The projects are thought through using curriculum that I have planned for the school year and that I collaborate on with colleagues. The skills I would like all students to acquire are embedded in the projects and designed to encourage mastery in the use of such materials and media as pencils, paintbrushes, markers, scissors, stencils, paint, ink, clay, paper, and fabric. The theme work during whole-class art is a whole-school connection that fuels the concept of shared learning, momentum, and story.

In addition to this hour per week is a time referred to as "open studio." During this open studio block, children arrive in the art room and get to choose how they will spend their time. Any class in the school can send two or three students, and if there are not too many students in the room, four can be sent. Children usually come to the art room excited and knowing what they would like to do. I always have paper, pencils, scissors, and tape at the ready for any project. I make a variety of small books for students to use; they like to make pouches that close with a string that they can put these books in. Hand sewing small projects, beading necklaces and bracelets, and making earrings are all favorite activities for this period.

There is a happy buzz of activity, and I have an opportunity to meet individual needs and get to know what inspires a student and stimulates his or her process. The setting lends itself naturally to supporting varied needs and learning styles, and I do encounter a wide developmental range of learners. The older students use this time to work on drawing skills that require focused attention on pattern, line, and design. With careful looking, a still life comes alive and techniques are explored and exercised.

The goal for the use of this open studio block in the schedule is to provide free time across a developmental range of ages and learners. Attendance by a broad spectrum of our school's population of students helps support cross-age connections, and the activities support imagination and play. I like to see different age groups working together, side by side. I help support this wide range of learners by facilitating their choices in art making, offering materials that serve many different levels of competency and leaving ample time for imaginary play and discovery. I can work one on one with students, giving feedback while supporting the whole classroom broadly. In any given open studio you will see a small group of older students drawing, painting, and beading (depending on the time of the school year) and some younger students playing with driftwood, branches, shells, rocks, and sometimes blocks or with an animal collection (which once belonged to my daughter). They are often busy creating nooks and crannies for the tigers, lions, and bears. Children play in groups of two, three, or four, negotiating the sharing of play animals, trains, trucks, and other objects.

Playing with the trains and wooden train tracks is another favorite activity. Children put the tracks together and make elaborate designs that weave in and out across the floor, over rugs, and under tables. Every time they are constructed the design is different. Toolboxes, wooden blocks, and wooden trucks are also available to the children. I have a few puzzles in baskets and there are always books placed and scattered around the room. Different types of seating are available, including a wooden rocking chair, a child-sized bench, small chairs, medium-sized chairs, and stools. Students are encouraged to get comfortable and play on the side of the room that has low-pile rugs and pillows with manipulatives stored in baskets against the far wall; students on the other side of the room work on their individual projects at tables.

I build into the schedule time for the display of student work, which changes with theme and work creation/production. My goal for display is to invite an audience and inspire and honor both the process and product of art and its making. It helps to prepare students in our 8th grade for the visual art portfolio and performance requirement. I invite our 8th-grade students to spend lunch and recess once a week in the art room to add time to their schedule for the preparation and practice of this performance expectation. Tapping into a wealth of creativity and expertise, our school's adult community act as mentors, helping to guide students in their performance goals, giving feedback and encouragement. I help support students interested in Boston Arts Academy visual arts portfolio and audition requirements. Encouraging those students to use open studio and occasional recess time and to work outside of school, I help them build a strong visual art portfolio.

WHOLE-SCHOOL THEME AND COLLABORATION

When I am planning curriculum, I look at the whole school year, not just a singular theme. I plan for a yearlong experience that I am trying to frame with experiences that flow into each other. I spend some time crafting curriculum/study that segues seamlessly into another. This way the journey of discovery and study continues—one study doesn't end abruptly; the learning continues down another avenue and deepens. I look for a thread that weaves throughout all our yearlong themes and creates connections, a layering effect or deepening of meaning of subject (a story or tapestry). While our habits of mind—Evidence, Viewpoint, Connections, Conjecture, Relevance—are exercised, our habits of work—Forethought, Perseverance, Production, Reflection—are also cultivated. As we are learning and producing, there is always something to see, a question being asked, a discovery being made that is apparent and accessible to the viewer of the art, the learner, and the teacher.

This work we do together is borne out of seeking the truth about a subject, our human history, each other. It's accepting each other's differences while we work together side by side to unravel the past and dwell in the present. It's making the best use of our time to affect the future in a positive way, not to continue destructive cycles, but instead to create change through knowledge. The setting of the stage for this learning takes time and thought. This work gets shaped and shared in many ways throughout the school year and over our summer break. We have committed to creating our own curriculum that is guided by essential questions and a common understanding about learning and teaching in a progressive pilot public school. Our time commitment to this work is essential for building connections with each other and collaborating on curriculum development. We have opportunities built into our workweek to give feedback to one another through curriculum shares and resourcing during professional development sessions. This work we do is passionate and demands dedication and a creative spirit.

VOICE, RESPONSIBILITY, RELATIONSHIPS

Education is not preparation for life; education is life itself.

—John Dewey

My role as an artist, teacher, and community member in our school is not one I take for granted. This is not a role that calls for complacency or martyrdom. In order to be present in the shaping of this process, I need to be constantly seeking truth in practice and thoughtful communication that challenges the status quo of traditional education. The relationships I have developed with colleagues, students, and families have required time to build and trust.

My voice is encouraged and expected in conversations about our students, our school, and our community, and with that voice comes responsibility and engagement. In my role at Mission Hill I have been asked to brainstorm with classroom teachers about projects, activities, and extensions for theme work. From sharing resources to making myself available to colleagues and giving constructive criticism and feedback, I participate with other staff members as we choose to work together to create and collaborate around curriculum. We come together at the end of the summer and have curriculum shares that we elect to attend. Each is an hour long and every classroom teacher is expected to share out a theme curriculum plan or framing question. During this time several questions are asked in a variety of ways to help flesh out ideas and implement practice.

Over the years I have acquired many resources such as books, art supplies, and assorted artifacts. These are the tools of learning, and I have plenty to share. I help to guide the planning and implementation of project-based learning, with careful consideration placed on forethought, preparation, and participation. Being prepared is a big part of the work of teaching and learning and children know when you're not prepared. Lack of preparation leads to precious time wasted and is uncalled for in our practice.

Over the years I have collected and kept track of my work with students through images. I take numerous photographs and turn them into subject area slideshows. This works for me, since I am a visual person, and it gives me a quick and fairly organized way to construct a visual history of our school and its art. The images can be shared and used as a resource schoolwide, have informed my practice during planning for an upcoming school year, and tell our story through art.

EXPLORING THEME THROUGH ART

I hear and I forget, I see and I remember, I do and I understand.

—Confucius

This section is framed by excerpts from a newsletter I wrote 6 years ago during our "Ancient China" theme. It showcases the art connection and content schoolwide, addressing a broad developmental range of learners. I have pulled the newsletter apart, making comments after segments that are relevant to content and conversation.

Mission Hill School News

Volume 2, Issue 26
Exploring Ancient China Through Art

Dear families, students, staff and friends,
    Art reflects the values, lifestyles, and beliefs of people. In the art room we began inquiry into aspects of life in ancient China with calligraphy. Calligraphy is not only the writing of Chinese characters, but the art of written language in many cultures, like cursive, Arabic, even graffiti. Students instantly connect it to the study, inserting their own styles and interests into the words and proverbs they chose to paint, and in the way in which they chose to paint them.

Calligraphy was an ideal entry into the "Ancient China" theme. Students in kindergarten and 1–8th grades all experienced painting and making marks with brush and ink. A photocopy of Chinese characters was placed on tables around the art room. Every place setting at the tables had a bamboo brush, a shallow container of black ink, a folded napkin, and a white piece of paper. Tables were set up so every student had a workspace that could accommodate the fluid movement of their arm. Students could move freely with a follow-through stroke of their brush. We looked at the direction of the Chinese characters one by one (up and down, right to left), which I demonstrated at an easel situated in the middle of the room. Prior to this theme was the "Nature Study" theme, which produced artwork inspired by butterflies, flowers, birds, and the natural world. This segued naturally into the aesthetic of ancient China.

During our first 6 weeks of school, we make self-portraits and name art, getting to know one another or getting reacquainted after the summer break. We then follow that with something light in medium-grade pencil, colored pencil, and watercolor, and the pattern and detail of flowers and butterflies offers a great way to delve into process. It also provides an opportunity to have beautiful flowers in simple small glass vases around the room. During this school year we had dahlias from a neighbor's garden. He grew over 30 varieties—they were his pride and joy—and he generously shared them with our school. I incorporated the flowers into our life science study. The careful looking at a flower (observation) helped to train the eye, especially when it came to the detail necessary for much of our Chinese-inspired art. Curiosity stirred and the senses awakened. We all loved those dahlias, and it became a tradition for the school to be filled with these flowers upon the return from summer break.

> Not only did we learn from the form of art making itself, but also the physical practice provided a window into ancient Chinese culture. During art class we emphasized the importance of balance and peace while painting. The stage is set, black ink and brush awaits white pieces of paper, the room flooded with sunlight from huge windows while traditional Chinese music is playing low; we are ready. Once in a while the room is completely silent, the students totally focused in an almost meditative state.

During this study I played Chinese bamboo music and other traditional instrumental collections. I kept the music soft and the room had a quiet, focused feel to it, especially when students were painting with ink. The tables weren't cluttered and children responded to the simplicity of sound and space, creating a peaceful working environment. All students painted with ink; mistakes were part of the plan. Some students just marveled at the deep, dark richness of the India ink against the bright white paper, while others focused on mastering a single stroke of their brush to achieve the character that meant *tree* or *rain* or *sun*.

> The same brushstrokes and philosophy have been revisited again and again in Chinese-inspired brush painting, scrolls, lanterns, and fans. Learning the role of these art forms in daily life, ritual, and

decoration through research, stories, and visits to the Museum of Fine Arts has provided a vehicle to explore ancient China from yet another viewpoint.

Classes were taken to the nearby Museum of Fine Arts (MFA) to view its collection of ancient Chinese art and artifacts. The trips were self-guided and with many chaperones so we could go off in small groups and explore. I made small books with a few guiding questions on several pages, along with plenty of blank pages to make observational drawings in pencil. Some classrooms not only visited the MFA with me during a scheduled art time but often went back to view the collections with their homerooms or in small groups on different days at different times.

This study is so rich that it inspires many hours of careful consideration from all ages, about life, art, and our connection to nature. As we move further into our exploration of ancient China, the hallway and classrooms start to reflect our work. Lanterns hang overhead, celebrating the Chinese New Year. Shaped fans, inspired by those made of bamboo and silk, dance on the walls outside of classrooms. Folded-style fans hang in the art room and in the hallways. Chinese proverbs beckon us with their profound meanings written on hangings and hand scrolls, and this is just a taste of what's to come.

The lantern project became a vehicle for continued exploration and rendition of Chinese characters as well as the fine-motor use of scissors

Sample of artwork created during the "Ancient China" theme

and folding and cutting paper. The fan, with its history and artistry, was a great canvas for scenic landscapes and bold dragons, leading to further discovery of nature in art. We learned more about hanging scrolls and hand scrolls as students continued work with ink and discovered that such artwork was signed with a chop (seal, made from a small piece of rubber carved with a Chinese character).

Our older students refine their skill at brush painting on hanging and hand scrolls painted on paper (originally invented in China), with ink and watercolor. The promise of spring informs their art, as students depict the graceful arch of a tree, the pattern of bamboo, or a blossoming branch. The younger students discover the dragon in their hand scrolls, working together to make four-toed mythical creatures with silver and gold scales. We have plans to make Chinese opera masks and kites depicting birds, dragonflies, and butterflies in honor of national kite month, celebrated in April. There is so much to do and our excitement in discovery fuels the art-making process.

All of this art is a true celebration in learning. Students' enthusiasm for taking home a fan or pointing it out to you while it is on display shows success and joy in their journey to knowledge. All this work in the arts helps shape our students. It prepares them not only for creative expressions and endeavors, but exposes them to cultural diversity and human history. Taking time to really look at ancient cultures, we learn much about craftsmanship and the sheer beauty and satisfaction we get from making something with

Students help one another create face-fitting opera masks.

our hands. What we make with our hands reveals the content of our hearts. Art made in the middle school is saved for the 8th-grade presentations in May, and for the Art Show in June. All of this work tells a story about a student's time at Mission Hill. When young people make objects with their own hands, the lesson content becomes concrete and tangible. Personal and universal connections and a strong sense of pride are evident in the outcome. It is truly an honor to witness the process from start to finish.

This work, the product, represents both pride and time. When students are invested and engaged in their learning, the aftermath—the art, the product—is evidence of their understanding and translation of information. Speaking about medium and technique (the making) stimulates memory and deepens meaning for students and for us (the viewers). Sometimes such discussion is simply a vehicle for the sharing of likes and dislikes, conversing about texture, content, and degrees of contentment. The memory of the hands can help the mind recall.

During the Art Show, which is part of the 8th-grade portfolio requirements, students are asked to talk about process and product. Their artwork, hung gallery style throughout our hallways, is a reminder of the importance of this work. This artwork, collected from the 6th through the 8th grades, celebrates and validates the visual arts, not as decoration but as communication. During the viewing, the portfolio committee is asked to look for growth over time and the ability of students to take risks (to move out of their comfort zones). We come to know not only the role that art plays in visual communication but also how the student/artist speaks to process and symbolic meaning. This time carved out for looking and listening to students gives voice to how they see the world, digest experiences, and share with us. It is a moment to be remembered.

Mission Hill News

News from the Art Room
        The art room has been a hub of activity during our ancient China curriculum. I started the unit by having students attempt to paint Chinese characters in calligraphy using bamboo brushes and ink.
        From there the focus turned to scrolls. Images of elaborately hand-colored dragons adorn the horizontally hanging hand scrolls, and special chops (a type of seal) were made to "sign" the hanging scrolls, which suspend vertically on the art room walls.
        Attention then turned to fans and their significance in Chinese culture. Children learned that the fan was a major vehicle for art and was also a symbol of social status; only wealthy women carried

them as a decorative accessory. The array of both folding fans (which originated in Japan) and flat fans (which came directly from China) that have been decorated with various calligraphic designs is amazing.

Another K–8 activity that has been popular is one where small groups of kids were given quotes to interpret with illustrations and calligraphy on a special hand scroll. "As old as the mountains" or "happiness is boundless" are some examples of quotes that became beautifully illustrated "translations."

In addition to the unit work, younger students have made their own version of terra cotta soldiers from clay while Alphonse's 4-5 class created ancient Chinese fashions, which they presented in a special fashion show at last week's Friday Share.

I have taught "Ancient China" three times in my history as an art teacher at Mission Hill School, and every time I do I learn something new. Teaching in themes on a rotational basis provides depth for both students and the teacher.

Handmade Chinese lanterns

CHAPTER 8

Assessment
A Tool for Learning

Heidi Lyne

Construction of knowledge means that students build on prior knowledge
by organizing, synthesizing, interpreting, or explaining information through
original writing, conversation, or performance rather than simply reproducing
knowledge.

—Laurie Gagnon, "Ready for the Future: The Role of Performance Assessments
in Shaping Graduates' Academic, Professional, and Personal Lives"

The Mission Hill School has had from its inception well-defined graduation
requirements, consisting of an extensive portfolio presentation and on-
demand tasks in five subjects: English-language arts, mathematics, science,
art, and history. Students are also asked to present on their out of the classroom experiences, which include but are not limited to an apprenticeship
in grade 8. These presentations, shown before a committee consisting of
teachers, family, and a community member, are spread through the 7th-
and 8th-grade years. As the Common Core State Standards are adopted
and there is a growing demand for students well versed in "21st-century
skills," more and more schools are turning to similar forms of assessment.
In this chapter we will look at both formative and summative assessment
practices and will examine the Mission Hill School graduation presentations as exemplars for assessment of the future, well aligned not only to
progressive education but (though my Mission Hill colleagues would probably disagree!) also to Common Core and 21st-century skills.

Assessment is used for two purposes: to provide the teacher with ongoing data about what each child is learning, so that there is a constant inter-
flow between data and instruction (formative assessment), and to ascertain

what students have internalized after the teaching is finished (summative assessment). At Mission Hill, and in many other good schools, there is ongoing teacher assessment not only of academics but also of how the child is doing socially and emotionally, the child's interests and passions, her ability to present herself, to make friends, to cope with adversity. We want to know—who is this child as a human being? What strengths does she exhibit? What challenges is she dealing with? But for the purposes of this chapter we will be dealing with mainly academic assessment.

When Mission Hill School began in 1997, one of the first things we tackled as a staff was our graduation requirements. We knew that in order to graduate, children would need to demonstrate their readiness to do so, and that the graduation requirements would inform the teaching and learning throughout the grades. Debbie Meier began the school knowing that she wanted extensive performance graduation requirements, and in our first summer together and initial year of existence the staff hammered out the details of that summative assessment. We met with teachers and looked at requirements from other neighboring schools using these kinds of assessments: the Fenway Pilot School (Boston, MA), Cambridgeport Public School (Cambridge, MA), and Francis W. Parker Charter School (Athol, MA) were three that I particularly remember. We held a retreat devoted entirely to finalizing our own requirements, believing that in order to teach well in younger grades, we needed to know what we expected our children to know and be able to do as graduates.

While the development of this final assessment was going on, we teachers were using some schoolwide assessments in math and reading, developed by Brenda Engel, one of the school's founders and a professor at Lesley College. Children were taped reading and talking about what they were reading twice each year and were placed on a continuum based on the tapes and the teacher's knowledge of the child. Math interview questions, carefully designed to ascertain strengths and weaknesses, enabled us to place students on a continuum of number sense. The assessments were well suited to our overall philosophy—yet were not very useful to me as a teacher inexperienced in assessment. Although I dutifully taped my children reading twice yearly, and administered our math interview, I had no real understanding of how to use these assessments to inform my teaching; rather I viewed them as summative, showing what the children had learned.

USING ASSESSMENTS TO INFORM TEACHING

As an educator in my 60s, my history with assessment is probably fairly typical. I have spent years in education, and my thinking about assessment has shifted and developed as I have worked in varying environments and as assessment has gained prominence in the field. I began my teaching career in prekindergarten in the early 1980s, and assessment was not in my lexicon. In those early years my assessment consisted of informal observation. I was somewhat aware of what each of my students liked to do and was able to do, but I had no system, no evidence, and no real understanding of the teach-assess-reteach cycle. As I moved up in grades, first teaching a 1st and 2nd mixed grade and then a 3rd and 4th mixed at the Atrium School in Watertown, Massachusetts, I began to be more deliberate about my observations, checking to see if children understood, and looking at work to see where misconceptions lay and skills were lacking. I also began putting my students into situations where they sometimes had to demonstrate their knowledge by sharing work with classmates and families. Yet I still had little understanding of why it was important to know exactly what each student knew and had no clear systems for ascertaining this or for collecting evidence.

I began teaching 2nd and 3rd grades at Mission Hill thinking a great deal about teaching and learning, but not at all about assessment. Yet looking back, I realize I was by that point constantly assessing without knowing it. I designed the class so that most of the teaching happened individually or in small groups, while the rest of the children worked independently. Because the teaching was so individualized, I had a pretty good understanding of what every child needed. As I moved about the classroom while children worked independently on a variety of tasks, I conferenced with each child about what she or he was working on. To the two children writing a story without punctuation I might say, "It's hard for me to read your work because you don't give me any markers about where to stop and take a rest. What do you notice about the book you are reading that is different from the book you are writing? When you read, how do you know where to stop and start again?" Or to the student doing a computational math problem and adding instead of subtracting, "How do you know what to do here? What is the symbol that tells you?" When I worked with groups to introduce a new skill or concept I never had more than four children in a group in reading or math, so I was easily able to ascertain who in the group was mastering and who was struggling with what we were doing. I looked to see what children needed and helped them to discover it themselves, then made a mental note to check the next time I was with that child to see if he or she had internalized the new understanding.

My use of children's work to see what they needed was not yet named or fully realized but it was a kind of formative assessment. Formative assessments are systematically used on an ongoing basis by teachers to find out which students have mastered a concept or skill and which have not, or what the child is struggling with. The teacher then uses this information to reteach: individually, to small groups, or to the class. Formative assessments can look different depending on the school, but whatever the philosophy of education, they are necessary. Good teachers must know what their children know and don't know, must know what they wish them to know, and must ensure that they know it.

In more traditional schools formative assessments of some kind may happen whenever a skill or specific content is formally taught. Teachers often use do-nows, exit tickets, quizzes, or other paper-and-pencil tasks to ascertain what their students know. They may ask the children to give signals to show how much they understood, or write answers on whiteboards and hold them up during the lesson, or use clickers, or turn and talk to a partner (when the teachers choose particular children to listen in on). In these classrooms, formative assessment is continual and ongoing and deliberate. The data is kept systematically and used to be certain each child is learning what is being taught.

RETHINKING FORMATIVE ASSESSMENT

But formative assessment is equally necessary in an environment like that of Mission Hill, where children's learning does not always follow the traditional path of "I teach, you learn; I assess, you show me if you learned what I taught." Instead, at Mission Hill, children are constantly learning by doing—creating, writing, playing, collaborating in a project, delving into their own interests. The teachers learn what the children know by working intimately with each child and studying the work they produce. Teaching and assessing are intricately intertwined.

W. James Popham writes in his book *Transformative Assessment* (2008) that "formative assessment is a planned process in which teachers or students use assessment-based evidence to adjust what they're currently doing" (p. 6). The missing piece for me in my years at Mission Hill was the "planned process." I knew where each child was and how to push her or him at an individual level, but I did not keep track on paper and did not have an overall picture of what I wanted each child to achieve in his or her time with me. As a consequence, though the individual attention meant that most children moved beyond grade level in most areas, there were a few who did not progress enough, and there were some who left my class with gaps either individually or as a group. My 2nd- and 3rd-graders, for instance, were advanced in working with fractions and could multiply and divide adeptly but had no mastery of math facts or knowledge of traditional algorithms. There were also individual children I failed in some ways, who would have benefited from more of my attention in a systematic way. In addition to simply pushing on from where the child is, teachers must always have a deep understanding of what they want children to have learned or accomplished by the time they move on, and must continually assess in some way to find out if the child grasped these understandings and specific skills.

Other Mission Hill teachers were more deliberate in their assessment practice. I remember one Mission Hill staff meeting, 2 or 3 years into our work, when we decided to share our ongoing formative systems for keeping track of kids. Most teachers relied on observational techniques for ongoing assessment. Some kept sticky notes on a clipboard and recorded what they noticed, then later filed the notes by child. Some had checklists and noted when they saw that a child had mastered a particular skill, or showed evidence of particular understanding a concept or making a new connection. Some examined each child's work at the end of the day, looking to see what skills the child had mastered and what habits of mind he or she was using. I said I had no system but knew where each kid was, and I did a pretty good job of defending that knowledge when my colleagues questioned me. But that was the moment when I began thinking—do I really know? Is my usually disorganized and forgetful brain really keeping all this information? Is anyone slipping through the cracks because I have no system? Now, in hindsight, I think I really did have an exceptionally good memory for what child needed what, and I also missed some things and let some children down because of my lack of data. And as I work with more and more teachers I realize that this should not be the only way to ascertain what children know, for not many people have that kind of memory and there will definitely be things that get missed.

The systems used by others at Mission Hill were more reliable, not only because they were better organized but also because the data could be used as evidence for reporting out to parents. What is looked at and how is still up to individual or grade-level teachers, but formative assessment has now been formalized as an ongoing system involving observation, work sampling, and interviews. In addition, at Mission Hill teachers have always looked at children deeply on occasion, knowing that understanding one child in depth would aid us in knowing and teaching all our children. When we were puzzled, we did descriptive reviews, a form of collaborative thinking about a child developed by Patricia Carini at Prospect Center. This protocol uses a nonjudgmental observation and description of children's work and behavior to delve deeply into the child's strengths and struggles. This combination of ongoing classroom formative assessment and a more structured collaborative look at children ensures that teachers truly know their students.

CURRENT CLIMATE OF SCHOOL ASSESSMENT

Now, in most schools, assessment is paramount—so much so that one must question how much valuable time is being taken away from learning. Teachers pre-assess to know who needs the instruction, reteach when most of the class does not understand or remember the concept or skill, and form intervention groups to address particular children in particular skills, then re-assess the children in the intervention group. Children are constantly being assessed—from observational checklists, do-nows, reading records, and exit tickets to quizzes and ANets (a standardized test that gives immediate feedback to help teachers know what the gaps are). Teachers have been taught to ask themselves: What do I want children to understand or be able to do? When I have taught it, how do I know if the class as a whole grasped it? Is the whole class or much of the class missing some key piece of information or skill? How do I know which children have gaps and which have mastered the content/skills? And now, what do I do about it? This kind of assessing is successful in keeping track of finite skills learned within a traditional teaching structure: The teacher teaches something; the student learns it and can demonstrate that learning. Most tests, do-nows, and exit tickets check for this kind of skill acquisition.

The Mission Hill approach to formative assessment is more integrated into the daily learning experience and more holistic, and it does not detract from children's learning time. Teachers rely more on observational data and looking at student work. They assess as they work with the child individually, noting where the child is demonstrating new understandings and skills and where the same mistake or misconception is happening again and again. They look to see how the child is thinking and what habits of mind and work he or she is developing. They combine these ongoing formative assessments with consultancies with colleagues and the more structured deep dives of the descriptive review.

This kind of assessing works well within an integrated student-centered curriculum, but it can work well in any kind of school. Informal observational assessment and conversations show more about the child as a person and thinker than do the more traditional skill-based assessments, allowing the teacher to think more deeply about what it is that the child is grappling with and thus better target his or her response. Because much of the work is done by the teacher without the child (observing, looking at student work, descriptive review, conversations with colleagues), the class time remains time for learning.

GRADUATION PORTFOLIOS AT MISSION HILL SCHOOL

But where the Mission Hill School most stands out is in its final assessment, in which students demonstrate what they have learned in their time at Mission Hill in order to graduate. The purpose of summative assessment is to discover, after all is said and done, what skills, concepts, and knowledge the child has mastered. It is often used to determine a grade for the child. Although it is not designed to help teach a child, it can help inform the teacher about his or her teaching—what worked and what didn't; what can I change for next year? As with formative assessment, there are many kinds of summative assessment. Standardized tests like our Massachusetts MCAS and other state tests are summative assessments; they purportedly tell teachers what children have learned. End-of-unit or end-of-term tests are often given to students; these help teachers grade children and help inform them of what they need to teach better the next time they teach the unit or lesson. At Mission Hill, the final summative assessment combines portfolios, presentations, and on-demand tasks:

> Portfolios put the students at the center of the process: they are given the opportunity to thoughtfully prepare and defend what they have learned through demonstration, conversation, and written material. This process of presenting and defending one's work before a group of parents and teachers—experts in the adult world—is tangible, interactive and concrete, and has immediate and very real consequences. (internal Mission Hill document)

The Mission Hill graduation standards are a summative assessment used to determine if this child has developed the skills and habits of mind and work necessary to be a Mission Hill graduate. Content is less important. The belief is if children have good habits of mind and work, and good reading, writing, and math skills, they can and will find out anything they need or want to know. It is not what is studied that is important; it is the habits of mind and work that the child develops. Thus, these are the focus of the assessment.

The graduation standards combine elements of formative and summative assessment and are intricately intertwined with learning; much of the teaching and ongoing assessment is centered around preparing for these demonstrations. All work students produce is done with graduation requirements in mind. The child's early pieces of work in middle school serve as formative assessments for the teacher, who understands what is necessary in order to graduate and realizes what in the child needs to improve. In addition, time is spent in middle school redoing work. In an ongoing process, student and teacher look together at what the student has produced to determine what is needed in order for the piece to be portfolio-worthy. We found that as time goes on the student takes more and more ownership over this process, sometimes choosing to redo work several times to reach ever higher standards. A culture of effort equating with excellence develops in most children as they spend their middle school years preparing for portfolios. The message is, when something is not good enough, work on it until it is—you can do it.

The portfolio/performance assessment is extensive. In creating and putting together the portfolio the child, helped by his or her advisor, asks him- or herself a series of questions. Do I have all the pieces of work I need? Is each piece done to my satisfaction, or do I need to rework it? Does the work, together and separately, demonstrate the Mission Hill habits of mind? Can I show in my presentation that I know the information or have the habits of mind necessary to find out the information? Can I think, reason, take different points of view? Am I skeptical? Do I know how to assess truth of information? And, do I have the skills I need to succeed in high school? The committee judging the student's work and presentation does so using rubrics that clearly delineate what the school is looking for. The child's graduation depends on passing the portfolio. These graduation standards ask much more of children than do most summative assessments. I believe they stand out as exemplary and are a large factor in the success of Mission Hill students (Knoester, 2012; Gagnon, 2010).

THREE MAIN COMPONENTS OF PORTFOLIOS

The Mission Hill graduation requirements have been honed over time but retain the original three components: portfolios of work demonstrating skills and habits of mind, on-demand tasks, and a presentation and defense of work (held before a committee). Taken together, these requirements reflect content and skills children have learned, habits of mind and work the child has developed, and the child's stance as a learner and person as she or he becomes an adult.

Let's look more closely at these three components, and first at portfolio assessment. Portfolio assessment is at one level a demonstration of skills. Traditional examples of this kind of portfolio assessment are sheets of math problems, sheets of answers to factual questions, a five-paragraph essay (demonstrating those elements that can be scored by a computer), a leveled book with a running record, and perhaps a research paper that sticks closely to a model asked for by the teacher. Better portfolio assessments show more: creativity, collaboration, originality of thinking, ability to learn from reflection, and good work habits. These pieces of work may be written papers that have a developed thesis, math work that demonstrates the ability to choose and apply skills needed to solve a problem, meaningful student reflections, artwork, creative writing, and so on. There are many formats portfolio assessment may take but the common thread is that the portfolio demonstrates whatever it is we want to see in our students, be it skills, creativity, good habits of mind and work—or all this, as at Mission Hill.

The process of building and defending a portfolio at Mission Hill cannot be underestimated. There are five subjects in which students present; each has a portfolio component. In order to present a strong portfolio, students must first create the work. Teachers design the middle school curriculum to ensure that students will have pieces of work to choose from. The final assessment is intricately intertwined with learning in the middle school, and much of the teaching and ongoing assessment is centered on preparing for these demonstrations. Each assignment students do is viewed by both teacher and student as a possible portfolio piece; when work is returned to the student the teacher may comment that this may be a portfolio piece. Students must then choose the work they have done over the year (or years) that demonstrates the qualities they want to present, revise if necessary, and check that the portfolio as a whole meets the requirements of the graduation standards. This process alone is an opportunity for learning: It demands reflection, effort, and a deep understanding of the habits of mind on the part of the student. In addition, students are practicing and solidifying executive functioning skills such as organization and time management.

A second component of the graduation requirements is the actual presentation of the work, to a committee consisting of at least one family member, the subject teacher, the child's advisor (a staff member from another grade or arena in the school), a committee member who does not work in the school, and a child a year younger who has been assigned to both observe and help the presenting student through the process. In addition the child may invite a classmate or friend from outside the school. Seventh- and 8th-grade students spend at least an hour presenting and defending their work to this committee in each of the five domains, on several occasions. The audience ups the ante enormously for students and is a main factor in developing the notion that effort and perseverance are rewarding. These attributes have always been important in education, but have now become bywords in current discourse about education. If students are performing, if they are actually presenting their work to family, friends, and strangers, their effort level climbs. People care deeply what others think of them—in teenagers this is particularly true. Presenting taps into this, and most middle schoolers show effort at a level one rarely sees otherwise.

In addition, students prepare, with the help of a teacher, to present the portfolio. They practice presenting, working not only on the organization of the presentation but also on speaking skills, politeness, and body language. They practice answering questions the committee may ask them. All students, whatever their level of achievement, benefit from this process. All students make huge gains not only in their understanding of who they are as learners and in their abilities but also in becoming stronger and more confident human beings. Parents, committee members, teachers, and the children themselves notice this development over the course of the presentations.

On-demand tasks are the final component of the graduation assessment. Performance assessment means "multistep assignments with clear criteria, expectations and processes that measure how well a student transfers knowledge and applies complex skills to create or refine an original product" (Stack, 2014). Grant Wiggins writes, "Assessment should determine whether you can use your learning, not merely whether you learned stuff" (2006). On-demand tasks show what a student can do without help. Each component of the presentations serves to demonstrate the child's abilities. The on-demand tasks ask children to use what they have learned to create something they have never seen before. Before their presentation, they are given a task and a certain amount of time to accomplish the task entirely independently. In history, children are asked to write a short paper about an historical figure. They may use the library and computer to do research. In English language arts they are asked to write a persuasive essay on a topic they have not encountered before. They must present a point of view and argue against potential opposing points of view. In math they are given a complex multistep real-life-based problem to solve, and in science they must present a hypothesis and demonstrate how they would prove or disprove it, showing good scientific habits. Whereas the portfolio shows the child's best work, honed and polished, these on-demand tasks prove that the child can actually use the skills he or she has learned independently.

EDUCATIONAL BENEFITS OF MISSION HILL
GRADUATION REQUIREMENTS

The Mission Hill graduation requirements as a whole also hold other benefits. Mission Hill students develop executive functioning skills; they learn in preparing for and presenting these requirements that work habits—like effort, perseverance, organization, and timeliness—matter. When children present, they are graded on each piece of work and are often asked to redo their work and re-present (or, in the case of very minor issues, to pass it in to their committee without re-presenting). Students who are asked to redo work see that their classmates who put more effort into the work before presenting have passed and are finished. The constant refrain as students work to try again is, "I wish I had worked harder on this." And when they re-present, and their committee commends them on their work, they feel the great reward of pride in work well done.

Unlike standardized testing, which is of necessity geared toward the average student at a particular grade level, Mission Hill's performance assessments allow all children to demonstrate growth, no matter what their level of achievement. English language learners, special education students, and gifted students can all demonstrate how their thinking and learning has progressed. Portfolio/performance standards reward effort and good work habits as well as habits of mind. Standardized tests sometimes offer an alternative portfolio assessment, which is an attempt to find a just way to judge the growth of severely challenged special education students. But when all students are judged by portfolio, this alternative is not necessary. And whereas in an alternative portfolio assessment the teacher does much of the work, at Mission Hill it is the student who chooses or creates pieces for the portfolio, based on his or her interests, and it is ultimately the student who stands to defend his or her work, whatever the challenges.

Another benefit of this kind of portfolio assessment is that students are learning an enormous amount by creating the work needed for the portfolio. As Laurie Gagnon so ably articulates in my chapter-opening epigraph, students are constructing knowledge, not merely iterating it, as they do the work of making a portfolio. They are using and solidifying those very skills and habits that they must demonstrate in their work and presentation as they create and edit a large portfolio of work. This is truly student-centered learning; the assessment and learning are inextricably intertwined.

It is true that the Mission Hill assessment—a mixture of portfolios, presentation, and on-demand tasks—leads to and stems from a different kind of teaching and learning; thematic student-centered teaching invites a holistic approach to assessment. Yet I would contend that this kind of assessment is not only ideal for theme-based learning and progressive teaching but is a perfect solution to the conundrum of how to assess the acquisition of the Common Core Standards and the skills that will be needed in our future populace.

MISSION HILL GRADUATION REQUIREMENTS MEET EDUCATIONAL GOALS VALUED BROADLY

There are many opinions about what is needed in education today but there is growing agreement that our educational system needs to move toward more of what is being called 21st-century skills, or the four Cs: critical thinking, collaboration, creativity, and communication. Good work habits and executive functioning skills are also being emphasized by all who are thinking about education today. We must find better ways to assess these skills and habits. The very concept of a standardized test is antithetical to assessing the aforementioned skills. Although it is certainly possible to have standardized requirements, how can such things as critical thinking, originality, and creativity be measured by computers or by teachers asked to score using a rubric? True assessment, assessment that demonstrates both capabilities and ability to think, is complex. This kind of assessment has been going on at Mission Hill and to a lesser extent at other progressive schools for a long time. Why not look to these schools for the models for the future?

It is also important to note here that the kind of assessing done at Mission Hill is a model for high-performing schools in other countries. Indeed, much of what happens at Mission Hill and other progressive schools in the United States is not accepted in the United States as good educational practice but is viewed as a model for good education elsewhere in the world. I spent some time working with teacher education at the Francis W. Parker School in Athol, Massachusetts, and was struck by the fact that educators from the Netherlands came yearly to study what was happening both there and at Mission Hill as they worked to reform education in their country. Pasi Sahlberg, author of *Finnish Lessons: What Can the World Learn About Educational Change in Finland?* (2011), writes about this in a post on Valerie Strauss's *Washington Post* blog, noting that much of educational reform in other countries, including assessment practices, come from ideas generated in the United States:

> Without frequent standardized and census-based testing, the Finnish education system relies on local monitoring and teacher-made student assessments. A child-centered, interaction-rich whole-child approach in the national curriculum requires that different student assessment models are used in schools. Furthermore, primary school pupils don't get any grades in their assessments before they are in fifth grade. It was natural that Finnish teachers found alternative student assessment methods attractive. And it is ironic that many of these methods were developed at U.S. universities and are yet far more popular in Finland than in the United States. These include portfolio assessment, performance assessment, self-assessment and self-reflection, and assessment for learning methods. (as quoted in Strauss, 2014, p. 1)

There is agreement about the ultimate goals of education today; there is ongoing debate about how to get there. In their well-known work on teaching for backward planning, *Understanding by Design*, Wiggins and McTighe (2005) say that the goals are the first step—the next step must be designing the assessment that will show that the goals have been reached. The Mission Hill school assessment system stands as a model of how to assess the skills that will be needed for the future of our country. Other high-performing countries are moving toward this kind of assessment—why can we not move beyond the standardized test to embrace a summative assessment that clearly demonstrates what we need to know: who is this child as a person and as a learner? And have we as a school done our job in preparing him or her for the next phase of education and life?

REFERENCES

Gagnon, L. (2010). Ready for the future: The role of performance assessments in shaping graduates' academic, professional, and personal lives. Boston, MA: Center for Collaborative Education. Retrieved from www.ccebos.org/research /Ready_for_the_Future.pdf

Knoester, M. (2012). *Democratic education in practice: Inside the Mission Hill School.* New York, NY: Teachers College Press.

Popham, W. J. (2008). *Transformative assessment.* Alexandria, VA: Association for Supervision and Curriculum Development.

Sahlberg, P. (2011). *Finnish lessons: What can the world learn from educational change in Finland?* New York, NY: Teachers College Press.

Stack, B. (2014, October 16). Competency education: Frequently asked parent questions. *Connected Principals.* Retrieved from connectedprincipals.com\/archives /10935

Strauss, V. (2014, July 25). Five U.S. innovations that helped Finland's schools improve but that American reformers now ignore. *Washington Post.* Retreived from www.washingtonpost.com/blogs/answer-sheet/wp/2014/07/25/five-u-s -innovations-that-helped-finlands-schools-improve-but-that-american -reformers-now-ignore/

Wiggins, G. (2006). Healthier testing made easy: The idea of authentic assessment. *Edutopia.* Retrieved from www.edutopia.org/authentic-assessment -grant-wiggins

Wiggins, G., & McTighe, J. (2005). *Understanding by design.* (2nd ed.). Alexandria, VA: Association for Supervision and Curriculum Development.

CHAPTER 9

Building a School Culture of Learning to Educate Children . . . and Adults

Ayla Gavins

A STEEP LEARNING CURVE

When I joined the Mission Hill School staff 17 years ago I knew very little about progressive education. It was our professional development sessions that saved me from letting my lack of understanding and experience determine my teaching—the experiences students would have in my classroom. In one of my earlier years at the school we took a course with Eleanor Duckworth. One of our sessions with her involved observing a student who engaged with a math puzzle. We (educators) sat around the room fishbowl style observing and taking notes. We noted each move the child made and words that were spoken. Afterward, we shared our descriptive observations and had many questions. I don't think Eleanor or her assistant answered any of them. She just asked us more questions in return. At the time that was frustrating, but what we learned about learning through our own experience was valuable. There are obvious lessons about child development that we learned from the observation, but we also learned to find our own answers to our questions.

At a different session with Eleanor we were given simple materials and a challenge to make the objects sink or float. We studied what happened each time we made a change in our constructed floating or sinking creations. It was from this work with Eleanor and our team that I began to understand inquiry, my role as an observer, the time it takes for discovery, and that we are never really done when it comes to learning about anything. The longer an inquisitive mind spends on a topic the more layers about the topic are revealed. I learned this as an adult and it changed not only my teaching but also the learner I would become.

Inquiry remains an expected part of teaching and learning at Mission Hill. Our annual focus on scientific thinking through a science theme naturally brings this to the forefront of professional development. However, essential questions leading to inquiry are created for every theme we teach, not just science. A great question leads to an investigation that could last a lifetime. One of my favorite parts of our curriculum development is our sharing with one another essential questions about a particular theme. A thread emerges and a schoolwide essential question is born. The following set of questions was generated at a recent professional development session as we prepared for a study of the ancient kingdoms of the Nile: What makes a civilization great? Why is this civilization's contribution to others not known? Does power make us great? How do we know about our own history? From what perspective? How is the mobility of people affected by their surroundings? How does the movement of people affect change? How do we know what we know? How does the past teach us for today? Teachers genuinely pursue these kinds of questions right along with our students.

PREPARING TO SERVE STUDENTS WITH A WIDE RANGE OF SCHOOL CHALLENGES

The posing of open-ended questions for exploration, off-site learning, value placed on creativity, and application of ideas to real tasks engages a wide range of learners. The progressive nature of Mission Hill makes it more inclusive by design. Children who learn in ways not suited for traditional classrooms flourish, as do more typical learners. I learned a lot from my atypical students and became a much better teacher and human being because of them.

In 2006 our school was assigned a classroom of students who had significant needs beyond those of most children Mission Hill had previously served. Embracing this new student group beyond just including them meant that all of us (staff, students, and families) had much more learning to do, and quickly. The sounds, energy, and motions in our school began to change. The frequency of children's yelling, crying, and running increased. What gaps were there in our knowledge and skill set in our responding to our new students? Our image of what school should look and sound like began to shift, shaking up what a progressive school could look and feel like.

Empathy, an understanding of what message acting-out behaviors were conveying, learning about the unique barriers to learning that students had and strategies to address the barriers, and managing teams of people who come along with complex individual education plans (IEPs) were areas needing development. All of this required professional development in addition to the attainment of special education certification by all teachers. This was a priority, so we could trust and effectively support one another in the work we were doing with families and students.

To expand our skills we read articles and books, visited other schools, and had lengthy discussions. From each resource we took what was most relevant to our population and to us. Creating a school community that embraces others who have learning and behavioral challenges will always be a work in progress. We all know that working with people is never fixed but always fluid. If we behave based on the idea that each one of us is truly unique, not better or worse than others but just different, we are opened up to infinite teaching and learning opportunities. This of course is a challenge too. How does a person shed the image of teaching and learning that society has created? How does a teacher meet the needs of so many? When I think of these questions I am reminded of Deborah Meier's push for us to think about all the different contexts in which learning takes place. For example, parents often teach their children of different ages and abilities the same task or idea but in different ways. One child may teach another. A supermarket must be user friendly to the general public, accommodating all levels of physical ability and intellectual capacity. In each of these examples, everyone benefits.

TEACHING IN AN URBAN AND DIVERSE CONTEXT

Working for the benefit of everyone is something we think and talk about often at Mission Hill. This does not mean that everyone gets the same thing. Unteaching that idea to children who don't often recognize the differences between us can be difficult. A year ago our staff went to Detroit to attend the annual meeting of the North Dakota Study Group. That year the focus was on race. A tradition at the North Dakota Study Group is for participants to meet in affinity groups. We each joined a group that represented how we identify ourselves. There was a group for Black people, White people, for people who were biracial, older, younger. When our staff came back together one of the White teachers proposed that the Mission Hill White affinity group members continue meeting throughout the year. There was agreement. A year later the White women teachers met with White student teachers to relay the importance of the latter's recognizing the difference between them and their potential students.

Teaching in an urban district requires flexibility of spirit and open-mindedness. There are curveballs thrown our way and we often have to manage them with existing school resources. An understanding of many things, internally and externally, is needed to feel truly empowered as a teacher. The student demographic of Boston Public Schools is primarily Latino and African American. For a Boston Public Schools educator, understanding one's own racial identity is important, but there are other factors to consider as well. Mission Hill has a fair number of students who speak English as a second language, families without many resources, and some students who have not experienced the things that mainstream society places value on. Our staff has used our learning about how to communicate with families in ways that honor what they know and bring to the classroom. We continue to have open dialogue about race and attend professional development events to improve our teaching of English learners.

One thing we realized is that having a shared thematic curriculum was really helpful for learners of all abilities and experiences. We had already known that our students benefited from studying one topic for months instead of for only a few weeks. We also knew that when students encountered a topic from multiple places and people in the school they were able to make connections and deepen their learning. From an adult perspective, knowing what all the students are studying makes it easier to connect with the students' learning and to extend it. In addition, we saw that for students with learning disabilities, our having 3 months in which to study a topic, versus the 3 to 6 weeks that most teachers have for a unit, further benefited students. Fewer transitions gave more time to students who take longer to process and organize. The project-based nature of work done by students was helpful as well.

TEACHING AND LEARNING IN A CONTEXT THAT WE CREATE

We have to keep in mind that learning doesn't happen in a vacuum. Environment matters. Relationships matter. Whether a person feels judged matters. Yes, there are some professional speakers and presenters who are masters at creating a climate of trust and comfort in a relatively short amount of time. However, it is the ongoing trust among the educators in the school building that matters most. It's the trust that people have in one another that opens their minds to learning and keeps the learning going.

Our first session of professional development last year was dedicated to setting norms for the year. We asked, What do we need as individuals to learn in the group? What are our expectations of one another? The norms stayed posted in the room where we met most often. Without structures like norms or use of a specific format, for example, it's easy for relational issues to develop. Our staff, even with its changing members, has felt like a family, and just as happens in a family, we've had our share of heated discussions and unkind words. A set of stated agreements has been really helpful in keeping our relationships healthy and the learning on track.

The dedicated space for our learning matters too. Is the topic best addressed in a classroom? Outside? In the teacher resource room? In the library? Because the physical environment can enhance or derail our learning, the facilitator selects the space and informs us all where to be and when and what materials we need.

COLLABORATION

One person doesn't plan professional development; many do. Professional development doesn't look one way and no one person knows it all. Professional development leaders at Mission Hill are generally the teachers who plan in partnership with a colleague or a team of colleagues. A team allows space for someone who is expert in an area to work with someone who is newer to thinking about a particular topic but wants to know more. The styles of different teachers or presenting teams comes through as they lead us in our learning. At the end of the session participants fill out a feedback form that the presenters read. This shared responsibility for adult learning and support for leadership roles is an important part of being a teacher at the school.

Professional development leaders vary in a year, even on the same topic. During one summer about 10 teachers participated in an online math course recommended by one of our math teachers. When we returned to school she led us in conversation and used part of the coursework video to guide our thinking and shape our work for the year. Later in the year our math coach led another session. During that session she referenced similar ideas presented to us at the beginning of the year. The math team followed up by leading another session in the spring. The format of each math session was different, but each built on the prior session, giving us a holistic approach to learning how to become more effective math teachers.

OPENING LEARNING OPPORTUNITIES

In a school whose foundation is the use of habits of mind and habits of work, the learning of every member of our school community is considered. As we build environments for our students to learn in, families and staff have to learn a lot too. This partnership in learning doesn't happen without structure, care, and attention. Our school year begins with a listening conference. Teachers either make home visits or invite families in to talk about their children. The teacher asks questions and listens. The parent or caregiver does most of the talking. This time is all about learning for the teacher so that he or she can provide the best possible learning environment for the student.

Each week teachers write a column in the school newsletter, sent home to give families a window into the classroom life. On the cover of this publication is a letter written to spark thought about a particular issue. We want parents and caregivers to think creatively too. Throughout the year there are Family Council meetings, where staff and families come together to discuss issues related to raising children, understanding differences, fundraising, and other topics of interest. This may not be considered professional development by traditional standards, but every time I attend a Family Council meeting I learn something from the conversation. I look forward to them.

TEAM SPIRIT

I think our school tends to attract and invite people who see themselves as lifelong learners. One of our interview questions for teacher candidates is, How do you feel about creating your own curriculum? The responses to this question tell me a lot about a person's willingness to be creative and learn as they go. Our final question—What questions do you have for us (Mission Hill School staff)?—also gives me a lot of information. If a person asks about logistical details, about relationships, or about how the structures work, I am learning a bit about them from the questions asked. During the final stages of the interview process, the commitment to professional development at the school is made clear, so the person can choose wisely about coming on board.

Continual participation in professional development opportunities for educators at the school is what we expect of one another. This expectation was set in the early years of the school by Deborah Meier and the founding teachers when the first school-based contract, the election-to-work agreement (EWA), was written. The language in the EWA we sign today is very similar to the one signed 17 years ago. The commitment to professional development is still clear and in writing. It states the following:

Therefore, teachers will:

- be available above and beyond the students' schedules for individual and shared work—school-wide for curriculum study, self-evaluation, planning, collegial support and school governance. This includes hours before school or after students have left for the day (house meeting, business meeting and professional development), 7 days before students return to school in September, one week at the close of the academic year in June, 3 days during the summer of self-identified professional development (ideally taken with at least one other staff member), and at least one mid-winter weekend retreat to plan for the next school year. For the 2013–2014 school year, our professional development hours will be 184 (after the 36 contractual hours are subtracted). The staff may determine changes in the details described herein for an equivalent plan, involving approximately the same allocation of time. The staff will recommend appropriate forms of compensation to make this feasible.

- be involved in on-going professional development on behalf of the school, such as inter-class and inter-school visits, school workshops and seminars, forums conducted by the Coalition of Essential Schools and the Autonomous Schools Network, academic disciplinary associations and other relevant professional events.

PROFESSIONAL DEVELOPMENT THAT MATCHES THE PURPOSE

Several types of meetings take place at Mission Hill, each with a different purpose. One is for sharing information about things that affect the whole school and making decisions. We call this a business meeting. Our house meeting is a weekly meeting with a smaller group of colleagues and is used for feedback on practice, room design, and problem solving. An action team meeting is similar to a student support team meeting, which happens in most schools. This meeting is for problem solving when a student is not experiencing success at school. Age pair meetings also happen weekly, with colleagues who teach the same age group; others would call it a grade-level team meeting. No matter what the focus of the meeting, adult learning is happening. Participants are learning about content, how to have asset-based conversations about children when they challenge the most, and how to improve the experience for children in the school and in the classroom. The questions that are posed during the variety of meetings we have get us to think, reflect, and try new things.

The best examples of professional development in the more formal sense in which learning objectives are clear for teachers happen in a variety of formats. One year we all took a course taught by one of our staff members, a professor at a local college. Thirty minutes or so after our students left for the day we reported to a classroom in our school for instruction. We were in the twin capacity of both teachers and students. Because he knew us as teachers and learners and knew the context we were working in, he was able to use what we knew to teach us. He also was able to create relevant assignments for us. We were asked to document strategies we used, record communications with families, and reflect on IEP meetings. That course led to several teachers getting their special education license.

During one winter retreat a teacher mentioned the lack of information she had about an upcoming topic, "Ancient Kingdoms of the Nile." Colleagues chimed in with similar feelings. Someone offered to connect with one of our volunteers who also happened to be an expert on Africa. The volunteer was contacted and was thrilled to help us out. She made arrangements for our staff to have a full day of professional development with the director of the National Center for African American Art. At the museum was a replica of the tomb containing a Nubian king and objects left for his afterlife. As the museum director told one story after another we were glued to what he said, wondering what he might share next. We left that museum enthused and ready to plan.

Our literacy team asked all classroom teachers to collect a writing sample from students that represented a range of writers. When we arrived for professional development, the team asked us to arrange the pieces of writing by student age so we could see the progression of writers across the ages 5 to 14. We wrote observational notes and began to shape a visual and written narrative about the development of writers based on the collection. Our expectations for students and each other were affected that day.

TEACHERS AND LEADERS OF STUDENTS AND PEERS

Most of our professional development sessions are led by teachers in the school. I recall two sessions led by one teacher, Heidi Lyne, as particularly memorable. It was her enthusiasm in being a learner and sharing her learning with the rest of us that made her so electric. What she taught us 15 or 16 years ago are practices that we still use today. I remember when she introduced the descriptive review process to us. She had just returned from a 2-week summer institute at the Prospect Center in Vermont, where she was immersed in the process. Her excitement about it was palpable. She invited us into her classroom, and we, her colleagues, sat down around a table, unsure of what to expect. She explained the protocol we would use and gave us examples of descriptive language. She made us practice using descriptive language until we demonstrated that we knew what it was. I remember sitting there not sure of what she was even asking us to do but being captivated by her energy and paying attention just so I could be clued into this really great something. She presented one piece of student work to the group. We followed her directions and she coached us through. We trusted her, so we were open to this unknown journey. After getting a taste of the descriptive review process, several of us went on to more formal training and participation in the summer institutes.

Our professional development calendar is created at the end of each school year. Teachers reflect on the year gone by and note areas of learning that need to be better prepared for the upcoming school year. Examples of topic titles include "Constructing Our Spaces," "Meeting and Communicating with Families," "Organizing and Using Archives," and "How Do We Document Learning in a Project-Based Environment?" A few consistent components are math, literacy, and theme. Theme sessions focus on the development and implementation of whole-school thematic units. Our thematic units are taught on a 4-year cycle. For example, each winter we study one of four areas of ancient civilizations: "Kingdoms of the Nile," "Ancient Greece," "Ancient China," or "The Taino of the Caribbean" (see Appendix A for more details). Even with curriculum materials from the past in our hands, updating and creating new plans are always necessary.

FEEDBACK TO IMPROVE STUDENT EXPERIENCES

During the summer teachers write their plans for the thematic curriculum. In the days before school begins, teachers share the curriculum plans with one another. We use a protocol to share our curriculum ideas. To be sure that each presenter has a focusing question to improve the plan for student learning and that participants stay on track, we use the consultancy protocol (www.nsrfharmony.org/system/files/protocols/consultancy_0. pdf). We've tried a few different protocols, but this one has worked best for us at this stage of sharing. Presenters share what the focus of the unit is and articulate what help they hope to get from the group. After hearing what different curriculum topics will be presented, other staff members choose a presenting teacher to listen and offer support with warm and cool feedback. Each presenter has three to five colleagues listening and providing questions, inspiration, and ideas. The recipient of the feedback feels as though he or she has been given a valuable gift. Through this process of sharing ideas, participants not only learn about a colleague's curriculum but they also hear things that might inform their own curriculum.

Later in the school year as theme curricula are in midstream, smaller groups of teachers meet for check-ins and assistance during house meetings. We find the tuning protocol effective for getting feedback while the unit is being taught and there is still time to make adjustments. This protocol, like many protocols, can be adjusted to 30 minutes, making it easy to use when there is very little time. The National School Reform Faculty has a wealth of protocols to choose from that are open for public use (www. nsrfharmony.org/free-resources/protocols/a-z).

Prior to the launch of a new winter or spring theme, teachers volunteer to lead a professional development session to get the rest of our team jazzed up and informed about the upcoming topic. I recall one session just before a study of the Taino people. Four teachers received a grant from Fund for Teachers for travel to Puerto Rico. They went to Puerto Rico to study the Taino people. They went to the rainforest and a burial ground, witnessed a Taino ceremony, and met people who shared stories about this peace- and nature-honoring people. The team brought back masks, music, photographs, and stories that created a picture of what life was like long ago for the Taino. The teachers created a series of books for use by all teachers and students. Because the story of Taino people is not a well-known one in our part of the country, resources were difficult to find and had to be created. The team of teachers set up the art room with Taino artifacts, music, books, photos, and packets that they made to teach and inspire us about the upcoming theme. Teachers had time to explore the materials and resources in addition to watching an informative slide show created by the presenters. The team also offered time to their peers in order to support teachers in planning. They continued to feed information to us throughout the course of the curriculum.

STAYING ON TRACK WITH NORMS AND PROTOCOLS

I could go on sharing stories of rich, dynamic, and collaborative professional development. But what is important to emphasize is that there are structures in place that help make that happen. A staff that functions democratically and has positive working relationships, such as at Mission Hill, needs structured conversation. We learned early on that there were some real benefits to using a protocol or a timed agenda. When a very opinionated and talkative group of individuals come together it can be a challenge to stay on task, give everyone the opportunity to speak, and maintain a supportive learning environment. Protocols help the presenter get the message articulated without interruption. We also realized that norms for our time together were needed. These are the norms from one school year:

MHS Professional Development Norms 2013–2014

Start at 3:50; end at 5:20.
Maintain balance of discussion and production.
Provide feedback on feedback forms or verbally at the conclusion of the session. This feedback should be kind, helpful, and specific.
Be present and actively participate; no class work during professional development.
Notify the presenter and others when you will be absent.
Plan any session that you are leading and communicate to all beforehand (2 weeks in advance at business meeting). There may be exceptions to this as plans change.
A voluntary sign-up sheet for snacks will be created.
Be mindful of our time.
Be considerate of space.

As I mentioned earlier, one of our teachers, Heidi Lyne, introduced us to a descriptive review protocol for looking closely at children through their work. The descriptive review of the child is one of many types of descriptive review protocols. I recommend reading the book *From Another Angle: Children's Strengths and School Standards*, edited by Margaret Himley and Patricia Carini (2010) for a deeper description of the process. For us as educators and parents it's easy to talk about children. We could tell stories about our students for days. And yet there are elements of a child that we might miss without having some guidance for our thinking. The descriptive review protocol provides such guidance for us. It requires us to think about the way a child speaks, walks, and engages with materials and space in the classroom. It requires us to think about whom the child is friendly with and which adults know him or her. Preparing a child study (descriptive review of the child) brings to the surface what a teacher doesn't know about the student. When the process is complete, everyone who had participated has a better understanding of the child.

It's amazing how a person can feel the presence of the child when the student is not in the room. Afterward we all feel more connected to the teacher and to the student. This plays out in our interactions with both. In fact, because we want to support and encourage this work, Mission Hill School has hosted a national conference focusing on descriptive reviews and the work of the Prospect Center, founded by Patricia Carini and colleagues.

PERSONALIZED SUPPORT

Whole-group learning, such as when the entire faculty meets before a new theme launch or small-group learning through a descriptive review, complement our peer support and two-to-one professional development through coaching and evaluation. Mission Hill has a peer review system that was created by Brian Straughter in the early years of the school. In the peer review system each educator is observed by at least one peer several times throughout the school year. The educator being observed meets with the observers, shares goals, and debriefs the observation with the observer. In addition to discussing observations, the team talks about student work.

This type of ongoing discussion of practice has benefits that are different from those offered by whole-staff professional development. It's personal and geared toward the specific goals of a teacher. Sometimes an individual has the same goal as a team of peers has. There may be a team professional goal or team goal around a student or group of students that each teacher is responsible for carrying out. We take time to write our goals together at the beginning of the school year.

One year the teachers of 6- to 8-year-olds shared a goal around increasing student facility with numbers, particularly using combinations of 10 to solve problems. When the team members planned together, they put their energy into sharing strategies and taking feedback. When peers who observed made visits, it was easy to see how the joint goal boosted the effectiveness in the classroom. However, the conversation and feedback happened with individual teachers.

Peer review works well only if trust is present. When feelings of mistrust arise, they have to be dealt with. Mission Hill has a process in place if an educator feels misunderstood, feels hurt in some way, or is in unresolved disagreement with others. By nature of being human, we disagree, hurt the feelings of others, and do other things that can be damaging. Having a public and accessible way of resolving issues is helpful in general and necessary for a learning community. At Mission Hill the first step a person must take when feeling frustrated is to speak to the offender about it. If that's hard to do the person may get help from a colleague to facilitate addressing the matter. Unresolved issues can cause rifts and snags in the adult community that derail learning.

INCLUDING EACH OTHER TO BUILD ON EVERYONE'S LEARNING

Involve as many people as possible in the adult learning community and trust grows within it. To do this it is helpful to have different ways of coming together. For example, Mission Hill educators spend one week together before the school year begins and one week together at the end of the school year, not just meeting during the year, when schedules can conflict with participation. This time is fully inclusive of everyone who can attend. We schedule the time together 6 months to a year in advance. These full days allow us to go deeply into topics that would get shortchanged if we tried to unpack them after school during the year. Agenda items are collected from staff members and I do the best I can to pull the topics together in a cohesive way. This year we will spend a full day learning about children who have experienced trauma. The Boston Public Health Commission will lead this professional development. We will spend 2 hours learning how to write IEPs. Our learning coach will lead this session. Another 2 hours will be spent discussing assessment at our school. This conversation will be led by a teacher. The time we spend together is truly a gift, and I don't take a single moment for granted. I am aware that at most Boston public schools teachers don't spend more than 40 hours of a school year in whole-staff professional development. Mission Hill teachers spend about 180 hours accomplishing work together.

It's an interesting time we are in. There is so much information available to us about adult learning. Books such as *Professional Learning Communities at Work* by Richard DuFour and Robert Eaker (1998) and articles have created buzzwords throughout the teaching profession. Despite all the information available to us, many professional development sessions begin with a presenter who says something like this: "I know this isn't best practice, but I have a lot to share with you and not much time." And so it goes. Participants are held captive, learning very little and maybe getting some other work done during the professional development session. I've endured many of these kinds of sessions in my career. After teaching for 12 years and getting my start as an administrator in another school, a large traditional school, I had lots of ideas about professional development in addition to everything I read.

When I entered the role of principal I had taught at 3 different schools, urban and suburban, large and small, progressive and traditional, with 1st-year teachers, teachers who had just crossed over the 5-year mark of experience, and others who were close to retirement. My experience learning with and from adults was pretty varied, but the main ideas in each setting that led to teacher and administrator satisfaction were pretty similar. Just as children should be at the center of their learning environment, teachers should be at the center of theirs. What does the use of a teacher's time look like? How will the use of minutes be most effective and rejuvenating? Where is the teacher voice? Where are teacher leadership and expertise? How is new learning connected to existing ideas or practices? Uses of Mission Hill School's habits of mind are helpful when planning professional development for adults. That means topics that are relevant to them and presented in ways that connect to their prior knowledge with room for active participation and engagement. Bringing those ideas to an existing structure that was already constructed around best strategies for adult learning seemed intuitive. With all these things considered, the question, How does one go about planning for adult learning? is an important one to keep asking.

REFERENCES

DuFour, R., & Eaker, R. (1998). *Professional learning communities at work: Best practices for enhancing student achievement*. Bloomington, IN: National Educational Service.

Himley, M., & Carini, P. (Eds.). (2000). *From another angle: Children's strengths and school standards*. New York, NY: Teachers College Press.

CHAPTER 10

Teaching in Themes at Mission Hill and Beyond
Collaboration and the School Culture Connection

Emily Gasoi

The power to define the situation is the ultimate power.

—Jerry Rubin, American activist, 1938–1995

FINDING OUR STRIDE: EARLY YEARS AT MISSION HILL SCHOOL

It's 8:45 in my 2nd/3rd-grade class, and the room bustles with activity. We are in our 3rd month of studying ancient Egypt and students are spread out across the room working on a variety of projects, some pursuing their personal interests, others working on pieces of a culminating project—in this case a class play written by the students. Angelo,[1] a 3rd-grader sophisticated beyond his years, works on his ancient Egypt encyclopedia (all students will create one during this unit, but some will add information they find only when directed by a teacher, while other students, like Angelo, become completely absorbed in this project, writing and illustrating lengthy entries); at the table with Angelo, Sabina and Keith, their heads bent close together, are reading a text about life along the Nile 3,000 years ago. They help each other with words as they go. At one point they stop to point out something they've just read and laugh a little, then continue reading.

At another table, I conference with Henry about a historical fiction piece he's writing. In this meeting, we're discussing mechanics, where to put paragraph breaks to make his work more readable. In the meeting area, Bethany reads the narrator part from a play script that several students have written together. The play is based on environmental, cultural, and historical information students have gathered over 2 months of studying ancient Egypt. After several peer-critique sessions and feedback from me, the script is now ready to be transformed into a play. As Bethany reads, seven students run through the scenes, mapping out their actions and attempting to remember their lines without scripts.

As a founding teacher at the Mission Hill School, my assistant teacher and I captured these scenes on video during our first study of ancient Egypt in spring 1999. It depicts a particularly productive morning I'd come to find was typical of the final weeks of our in-depth studies, everyone working toward the common goal of completing projects to share with the entire school community, including families. Footage taken of work periods earlier in our study shows a similar bustle, but I am more present, introducing topics and materials, leading meetings to gather and share ideas for projects, checking in with students to make sure they are engaged with resources appropriate to their skill level and interests, assisting others who are having trouble finding their way into the subject matter. The early weeks of our themes involve a lot of exploration. Some students find what they're interested in right away, as with Brandy's obsession with hieroglyphic writing, which culminated in a dictionary and poems written in carefully rendered hieroglyphs, or William and Darnel's interest in theories of how the Great Pyramids were built, culminating in a series of related projects that included building a scale model of Giza out of sugar cubes, complete with small paper people and simple machines they might have used to stack the large rock slabs.

In the course of a thematic unit, many students complete several loosely related projects, or start one and then drop it to move on to something else. This was true of Sarah, a precocious, science-minded 2nd-grader who spent hours of her project time attempting to dissect the tiny body of a salamander she had found dead in the schoolyard. Following the ancient Egyptian tradition of removing the organs of the deceased before mummification and placing them in canopic jars, she made several tiny clay vessels she hoped would hold the salamander's innards. Unfortunately, because the salamander was so small she wasn't able to find the essential organs. She gave up on that project and ended up putting her energy into creating a field guide of flora and fauna that lived along the Nile. This kind of mucking about, exploring and trying things out, is an important part of the learning process that helps children test and develop their ideas and reinforces the notion that learning is about more than just getting things "right."

Some assignments were required of all students during each theme study. Class time was set aside for each student to keep a journal of their work for the day. In addition, all the students created an encyclopedia of information they learned and at least one written piece based on their research; the piece might be a historical fiction story or play, a book of poetry, a history text, a guide to some aspect of the environment or culture—as long as students incorporated their topic-relevant research and their wonderings, any format was acceptable. And, as much as possible, I integrated theme-related work into other subjects—studying scale, measurement, and geometry related to pyramids during math and simple machines or the study of rivers during science.

From a pedagogical standpoint, thematic teaching at Mission Hill is not seen as a tool for making academic learning more palatable for students. Rather, academic and other skills are taught in the service of conducting in-depth research on complex topics. Teachers help students develop valuable skills, as well as the habits of work and mind they will need to conduct research independently and with peers, and then to apply their knowledge to create works that will illuminate the topic for others. In order to do this, students spend time working independently, but they often must find others with whom to collaborate in order to bring their vision for a particular project to fruition.

Our Class, Our School, Our Community

There are multiple ways that the theme work teachers do in their classrooms carries over into the larger school community. Much of it happens organically through our commitment to making our work public. From 1997 to 2012, Mission Hill was housed in an old Jesuit high school with high ceilings and a long, wide corridor running from one end of the school to the other. We deliberately allowed work from our classrooms to spill out into the corridor so adults and children alike could witness works in progress. Footage included in the video clip I described at the beginning of this chapter features several students in the hallway outside our room, working on sets for the play that was being rehearsed inside. In this section of the clip, Karah, a petit 7-year-old with old-soul eyes, appears to be directing two other 2nd-graders, Bailey and Jenna, who are painting white birds flying over a blue river and tall grass, on a long piece of brown butcher paper stretched out on the floor.

Another student chats cheerfully with his painting partner, while another works alone, putting some touches on brown hills and stepping back to look at a picture in a book of ancient Egyptian murals before continuing. As they work, a constant flow of foot traffic from adults and students ranging in age from 5 to 13 pass by the set painters. Some glance at the work as they go, and some stop and comment or ask questions. At one point Donald, a high-energy 3rd-grader comes out from the classroom with what looks like a book he's making. He kneels down to show one of the painters something in his book in progress. They talk animatedly (though, unfortunately, inaudibly) about something on the pages. Then Douglas turns just as quickly as he came back into the classroom and the painter returns to his work. It's at once a very productive and a social scene captured in this 5 minutes of tape.

This kind of social, contextually relevant activity, so integral to thematic curriculum, is at the heart of learning at Mission Hill School.

Often the community comes together around our work in planned forums. Every Friday morning, the entire school gathers to share works in progress. Students from each classroom, from kindergarten through 8th grade, describe, demonstrate, or just plain show off their knowledge and their projects. Families are invited to stay for Friday Share, which also includes whole-school sing-alongs. It is in this weekly forum that a lot of cross-pollination between classrooms takes place. Students are often inspired or intrigued by work being done in another class and they are encouraged to go inquire further about what they have seen.

Another planned forum is the culminating event that concludes each thematic study. Every classroom invites families to participate in a celebration that includes displays of finished projects and performances that provide a window into students' thinking about the topic they have just spent months studying. For teachers, culminating projects are used to assess students' understanding of the content as well as a range of skills and habits of mind and work.

Is teaching through themes more labor intensive than more traditional instructional methods? In some respects it is, especially in the planning and introductory weeks of a new topic. It reminds me a bit of what I've heard parents of twins describe about the first months of caring for two infants—it feels like maneuvering inside a tornado: hectic, stressful, exhausting, all with a consistent undercurrent of adrenalin and excitement. But as the twins become more independent and interested in playing with one another, having two actually eases parents' load somewhat. "It doesn't feel as constant as it did when our first child was a toddler," a friend who has twin daughters and one older child once explained to me. "With our first, we were his go-to for everything. The twins have each other."

So it is with thematic teaching. In order for most students to become productively engaged in a long-term study, they need more intensive adult guidance up front than they might if they were doing routine and discrete tasks. But after participating in teacher-guided activities related to the topic, including sharing books, films, guest experts, fieldtrips, factual reading, and hands-on explorations, students inevitably become far more independent and interested in working with one another than they would otherwise be in a more traditional classroom setting. As my students became immersed in their own study, I was able to let them work independently, freeing me up to give more attention to individual student and group needs.

It is also true that planning a new unit requires a lot of attention even before it is introduced to students. This begins with teachers making time to conduct their own research on the chosen topic and allowing that learning to inform the kinds of resources one gathers. Of course, as with most things, planning and laying the groundwork for thematic units becomes easier with experience, especially if the same theme is revisited annually or triannually as is done at Mission Hill. As valuable as experience is, in my years at Mission Hill, I came to view my collaboration with colleagues, who were all equally invested in creating the best possible learning environment for students, as absolutely essential.

Schoolwide Thematic Teaching as Democratic Practice

When Meier wrote the proposal for Mission Hill School to become part of the Boston Pilot School Network in 1997, she included schoolwide themes as a key structural element. Underlying this decision was Meier's understanding of how to create supporting structures for a democratically run school in which teachers and students play an integral role in bringing the curriculum to life. That summer before opening the school I worked with my colleagues to fill in the curricular contours Meier had drawn. From her proposal, we knew we would spend approximately 3 months on each unit. One would be focused on an ancient civilization ("Far Away and Long Ago") and another on current events and 20th-century American history ("Near and Dear"), and then the third would be something we would choose with our students (this would later become a science study). My colleagues and I met for several weeks that summer in the echoing rooms of the yet-to-be-filled school building, at the Boston Children's Museum, and in our backyards. The meetings bubbled over with the anticipatory excitement of embarking on a great adventure with a band of spirited comrades. In retrospect, I realize that this intensive preparatory planning not only set a high bar for productive collaboration but was, in and of itself, an invaluable bonding experience for the staff that laid the foundation for a culture of almost fierce collegiality.

We Meet A Lot!

House meetings, whole staff meetings, extended retreats.[2] When teachers sign their contracts to work at Mission Hill School, they agree to meet together at least 10 hours a week, in addition to meeting for extended professional development retreats. Putting so much time aside to meet, on top of teaching full time, can seem daunting for new staff. But for most of us, our time with colleagues is rejuvenating rather than draining. It sustains our sense of professional engagement, our commitment to our work as educators and to one another as colleagues.

I remember keeping notes on students—*Sheila has really taken on leadership for creating the artifacts for our mock tomb; Gabby has started to be able to read her own and others' ancient Egypt encyclopedias; Keith hasn't yet found his place in this study, he wanders around the room spending 5 minutes looking through a book on hieroglyphs, 10 minutes observing what others are doing, etc.* I knew my house colleagues and I would take time at our weekly meetings to share these kinds of informal assessments of individual students. We compared notes, looked for patterns and standouts, areas where we should step back and where we should take things deeper, individuals who were thriving and others who needed more support; and we shared our strategies for addressing the various problems that arose. What we came to understand in those meetings was that no one was more knowledgeable about the work we were doing with the kids in our care than were we, and so our time to confer and share with one another, to air our misgivings, challenges, and triumphs, was invaluable.

BEYOND MISSION HILL:
EXPLORATION OF THEMATIC TEACHING ACROSS SCHOOL SETTINGS

In 2004 I left Mission Hill School and moved to Washington, DC, where I now work as a course instructor and instructional coach with a progressive teacher-training program. Part of my job is to mentor Pre-K to 8th-grade teachers during their first year in the classroom. Over the years, I have had the opportunity to work with dozens of teachers in a range of school settings, from progressive and no-excuses charters to traditional and innovative public schools. During my travels, I have not found another school like Mission Hill, where everyone engages together in deep study of one theme across grade levels. However, I have seen that there are many DC schools that do engage in some form of thematic study in grade-level teams or, at the very least, in individual classrooms.

Overview of the State of Schoolwide Thematic Instruction in Washington, DC, Public and Charter Schools

- District of Columbia Public Schools have developed thematic curriculum for each grade level that integrates language arts and the humanities, but schools use this feature of the curriculum to varying degrees.
- Many DC public and charter schools are organized around theme-oriented programs, such as STEM (Science, Technology, Engineering, and Math), Expeditionary Learning, and International Baccalaureate, among others that promote some level of shared vision among staff.
- All DC schools that currently engage in whole-school thematic instruction do so across grade-level teams (e.g., all 1st-grade classrooms might spend 6 weeks studying "friendship," while all the 2nd-grade classrooms study "heroes," and so forth). The kind of work that Mission Hill does, where the entire school engages

in study of one topic at varying levels of sophistication across grade levels, is not generally practiced (though one arts-based charter has considered trying the Mission Hill schoolwide theme approach. I'll discuss that further below).

- Even within schools where no structures were in place to support thematic study, individual teachers or grade-level teams often made time and space to initiate thematic work on their own.

Looking beyond Mission Hill School in this way, I was interested in exploring conditions and practices in a range of school settings that support or hinder the ability of school leaders and staff to actualize their goals related to whole-school thematic study. Toward that end, I collected perspectives on the topic from more than 2 dozen teachers I have worked with over the years who self-identified either as working in a school that practiced thematic instruction or as having used (or attempted to use) thematic units in their own classrooms.[3] Gathering data from a survey, individual interviews, and a focus group, I asked the 26 participants to describe their successes, challenges, and concerns, as well as their ideas about what factors were most important for successful engagement in whole-school or schoolwide thematic study.

Voices from the Field: Teacher Perspectives on Thematic Instruction

First, what struck me most about the 15 survey responses was, regardless of the school setting and the degree to which respondents felt they had been able to implement thematic study in their classrooms, there was absolute unanimity about its benefits to student engagement and learning.

Reflecting on your experience teaching skills and content through themes/units, rate how important you believe it is for students to engage in this kind of learning.

- 100% of the 15 teachers responding to this survey question indicated that it was *important* (3) or *very important* (12) that their students engage in theme-based learning.

It is difficult to quantify the benefits of this kind of teaching, but all the teachers participating in the survey agreed that the benefits were many and that enhanced student engagement was immediately apparent to them.

Reflecting on the most successful theme/unit you have done with students, rate the overall level of engagement during this study.

- Of the 15 teachers who responded to this survey question, 100% indicated that overall student engagement was *high* (8) or *very high* (7).

While a majority of teachers responding to the survey indicated that all the proposed conditions were important to their ability to implement thematic teaching in their classrooms, they all rated collegial collaboration as the most essential element. In fact, responses from the survey, focus group, and follow-up interviews mirror the sentiments of teachers from Mission Hill School regarding the importance of collaboration in facilitating their ability to actualize their vision of thematic teaching.

Which of the following factors (if any) have facilitated your ability to implement thematic study in your classroom?

Administrative support	53% (8)
School resources	73% (11)
Collaboration with/support from colleagues	86% (13)
Professional development	40% (6)
Teaching experience	73% (11)

Note: Teachers responded to all applicable options.

What Teachers Need: Collaboration and a Mission

A finding to emerge from this study was that teachers who claimed to enjoy a high degree of productive collaboration with their colleagues all worked in schools that had a strong, unifying mission. For example, 5th-year teacher Ronald, who works in a public middle school serving mostly high SES (socioeconomic status) students, explained, "Most of what we do is theme based and [grade-level teams] do everything together. This is primarily due to us being an international baccalaureate school. It creates commonality among classes and makes interdisciplinary lessons somewhat easier."

Other teachers who expressed satisfaction with the level of collegial collaboration at their schools all work in two charters, each of which has developed a strong culture around its respective foundational mission. Several of these teachers work at George Washington, an expeditionary learning school that prioritizes collegial collaboration among grade-level teams. As Spencer, a teacher who had been at the school for four years, explained:

We are an expeditionary learning school, so the expectation for every teacher is that you are teaching through project-based and experiential learning. If you're not doing that it's a very big problem for the administration. So it's not an accident that it's all co-planning and Interdependence with your [grade-level team]. I think there's a lot of peer oversight to make sure you're carrying out the expedition with fidelity.

The other school, Great Expectations Arts Integrated Charter School, a progressive school in its 3rd year serving mixed-income students, had not yet set up structured times for teachers to plan together. Despite this, teachers have consistently met on their own volition in mostly grade-level teams in order to share practice. Most recently, Nancy, a 3rd-year teacher, initiated a meeting to try to address the lack of continuity she perceived in the curriculum across grade levels. Nearly every teacher in the school attended the initial meeting and then continued to meet weekly for 2 hours after school over a 2-month period. Nancy and one of her colleagues, Clarisse, both attributed this initiative and dedication among teachers at Great Expectations to common respect for the school's mission and philosophy and a shared responsibility for all students in the school, not just for one's own classroom.

What Great Expectations teachers discussed was improving teaching and learning by creating more continuity across grade levels. In the course of their discussions of how they might do this they watched clips focused on thematic study featured in the *A Year at Mission Hill School* video series by Amy and Tom Valens. Nancy describes her and her colleagues' reaction to the Mission Hill shorts: "We like the idea of being aligned and energized by how much we do together. When we looked at MHS [clips] . . . we wanted to do that—we wanted to study something all together. Especially the 'Long Ago and Far Away' theme, or thinking about *place*—we are moving the school location next year and figuring out how to integrate that into the curriculum, and it's something everyone in the whole school community will be able to relate to."

School Highlight: George Washington Expeditionary Learning Public Charter School

---

School Demographics

43% Hispanic
41% African American
7% White
9% Other
16% Special Education
70% free/reduced-price lunch

Walking through the halls it might not be immediately apparent that there are themes, because the student work on the wall spans a wide range of different topics—drawings of butterflies on the 1st-grade bulletin board, numerous unique marble shoots made of recycled materials on a table labeled "force and motion" outside the 2nd-grade classroom, colorful rainforest fact books beautifully displayed outside the 3rd-grade classrooms, and so on, each grade-level clearly engaged in project-based learning. What I came to understand while coaching several teachers at George Washington over the years is that each grade-level team studies multiple thematic units, or expeditions, together, each expedition lasting approximately 12 weeks. The work that is displayed outside classrooms represents work from all the students from a grade, not just one classroom.

George Washington (GW) has organized the school vision and practices around the principals of expeditionary learning (EL). Learning at GW takes place in the context of themes that, as much as possible, involve students interacting with their communities and the world around them. Similar to Mission Hill, students at GW work on culminating projects and each grade level invites families and the community in to view their work at several Learning Celebrations throughout the year.

There are several practices that support teachers' ability to actualize whole-school thematic units in the form of expeditions. For example, time has been set aside each week for teachers to meet in their grade-level teams, as well as to come together as a whole staff once a week. Teachers don't come up with expedition topics, but they do develop them together with their grade-level partners.

Another important factor is the sense of shared responsibility that the school leadership instills in the staff. As one 8th-grade teacher, Shelly, explained, "There's a lot of trust from the administration that teachers are going to come up with a strong expedition for students. As a teacher [at GW] the freedom to make the expedition your own is great, but we also really need support and guidance [from our administration and colleagues], like, 'Let's look at these plans and see how we can tweak them to make them more aligned with our school mission.'"

Finally, the administration provides resources in the form of support staff (each grade level has an instructional coach, a special education coach, and an English as a second language [ESL] instructor), materials for their expeditions, the freedom to go on fieldtrips where and when they see fit, and money to spend at their discretion. Some teachers, including Shelly and her 8th-grade colleagues, received extra money from the administration to work on improving their expeditions over the summer.

GW teachers also described obstacles they experienced, both in meeting their goals of integrating their own and student interests into the curriculum and in meeting the school's mission of offering students contextualized learning experiences by teaching all content through the lens of broad and relevant topics. Spencer, a 4th-grade teacher at the school, explained:

> The big difference of EL [Expeditionary Learning] and inquiry—expeditions are already set. It can be nice for teachers because then we can [teach

the same expedition] multiple times and perfect it a little more each time. It's difficult to be flexible—like if a kid gets interested in something else related, but not quite what we're doing, we can't just go off and let them take it where their interests are because [expeditions] are predeveloped according to the [content] standards and the EL model that's already laid out. I have tried to make [my units] inquiry based but it's very difficult. So I definitely feel somewhat limited by the expectation model.

Another obstacle that GW teachers have encountered in the past few years is related to a change in demographics. With an infusion of more low-SES and ESL students, their test scores have declined. In response, the administration has shifted some attention away from expeditions in order to prepare students for testing. Spencer spoke for all her colleagues working in testing grades when she expressed her frustration:

> In early days there wasn't a focus on testing at all. I was never asked to teach to the test or do any test prep [with my students] or move my schedule around or do anything different than what was expected with expeditions. . . . But in the last few years the demographics have changed [there are more poor, minority students] and so has the emphasis on testing. So . . . there no longer feels like there's a clear vision. I've been asked not to do my expedition in the spring and to do test prep instead, so I think the vision between . . . what my school holds dear and testing— there's been a lot of tension around that in the testing grades lately.

Echoing the sentiments of their colleagues who work in theme-oriented schools, teachers who worked in schools where thematic study was not prioritized were even more adamant that collegial collaboration was essential. This was especially true for new teachers who had hoped to engage students in contextualized learning in their classrooms. Alison, a 1st-year teacher who works in a traditional public school, explained that while grade-level team collaboration is mandated by the principal in her school and time is set aside for weekly meetings, there was little motivation among her colleagues to work together.

"It was very superficial," she explained. "It was hard enough to just get [my team] to talk about what standards they were teaching or what read-aloud they were going to use. There was no way we were together enough to plan a whole theme." This led Alison to skim over much of the thematic units embedded in District of Columbia Public Schools literacy curriculum. "I was so scared about being a new teacher, I just didn't feel like I was able to implement a whole theme on my own. Thinking ahead to next year, I could imagine doing inquiry-based projects but I can't imagine doing theme without support from my team."

First-year teachers across different school settings expressed similar concerns over the lack of collegial support. For example, while Alison works in a Title I school, Karen, a 1st-year teacher who works in a public school located in one of the wealthiest zip codes in the city, also spoke about the lack of collaboration as a significant hindrance. Karen explained that her school's high test scores relieves pressure on the principal, who in turn allows teachers a high degree of autonomy in the classroom, as long as student test scores don't slip. But she still feels it's too difficult to delve into in-depth study on her own:

> I somewhat feel like I have the freedom to do themes, but I don't have the support or experience. There's no collaboration at my school. There's a real *my classroom, my castle* mentality, and I need some guidance to make this happen. There are just too many demands and it's very difficult to then plan a thoughtful and meaningful unit based on the standards and all the 90 billion other things we're expected to incorporate, not to mention what you or your students might be interested in studying.

More experienced teachers also felt that lack of collaboration had hindered their ability to take their thematic units as far as they would have liked, but they seemed to be able to create pockets of in-depth study in their classrooms. For example, Nina, a 3rd-year teacher working in a traditional, mixed-income public school where collaboration was not the norm, explained that the units she did were her and her students' favorite part of the curriculum. "But I could have done so much more if I'd been able to work with other teachers. We never went as far as I felt we could have had there been more than one teacher planning everything."

Overview of what teachers said they needed . . .

- Time
- Guidance/professional development
- Collaboration with colleagues
- Trust from the administration (especially the leeway to take risks and make mistakes)

Overview of what teachers said school leaders need to know . . .

- Prioritize vision over external mandates
- Acknowledge that the kind of learning experiences offered by thematic units is not only for "some" kids
- Create opportunities for teachers to learn from colleagues in their own and in other schools
- Provide support and guidance, especially for new teachers
- Create structures and guidance conducive to authentic collaboration
- Balance structure with autonomy

In addition to these exceptions, there were some pockets of collaboration within schools that were not otherwise conducive to strong collegiality, but these depended on an experienced team leader and the targeted support of the administration. For example, Jason, a 1st-year teacher at Big Dreams, a no-excuses charter school serving low-SES, African American students, explained that he was lucky to be part of a grade-level team with a particularly skilled lead teacher. Because this teacher had earned the respect of the administration, the principal also supported the team's efforts to engage students in extended thematic units. Lisa, another 1st-year teacher working at Big Dreams had a dramatically different experience, with little motivation among her grade-level colleagues to work together, and no support from the administration. Both Jason and Lisa agreed that Lisa's experience was more representative of the state of collegiality at the school in general.

The administration at Chambers, a public school that has adopted some progressive practices, recently decided to transition the school to teaching science, literacy, and humanities through integrated themes by grade levels. The administration has left it up to each grade-level team to figure out what their themes for the year will be, but they do not have a choice of whether or not to participate in the plan. Teachers I interviewed from the school reported that they felt as if they had been handed a "friendly" mandate without much support or guidance from school leaders. A clear lesson to emerge from this research is that the success of schoolwide thematic teaching depends on buy-in from both teachers and administrators.

School Highlight:
Chambers Public School

School Demographics

74% Hispanic
10% White
8% African American
7% Asian
11% Special Education 75% Free/Reduced-price Lunch

Chambers Public School is located in one of the most demographically diverse areas in the city. Despite this, it has only been in recent years that Chambers has begun to reflect this diversity, since the schools chancellor made it a priority to attract more affluent families to the public schools. Some schools were strategically chosen for "revision," Chambers among them, and the leadership was systematically replaced with more progressive leaders who might attract more middle-class families to the school.

When I interviewed Hannah, a 4th-grade teacher who had just completed her 2nd year at the school, she explained that she had been chosen by the principal to be on the school leadership team, composed of administrators, learning specialists, and two teachers. During the previous school year, the leadership team had decided that all classrooms should engage in integrated, thematic instruction. The principal asked that the team help actualize this plan for the following school year.

I asked Hannah to describe what supports she believes need to be in place in order to successfully launch the school's transition to thematic teaching, as well as what possible obstacles she anticipates based on her knowledge of the school community and culture. One of the primary supports that she believes is already in place is the stance of the school leadership, which she described as very open to new ideas and who grants teachers a relatively high level of autonomy to try things out in their classrooms. Related to this, Hannah feels she has a strong line of communication with the principal and good relationships with her grade-level team, including instructional coaches. Perhaps most important, there will be a weekly meeting time for grade-level teams to meet with instructional coaches—she believes this structured planning time will be invaluable for supporting collaboration around practice, including the common theme work they will be expected to implement beginning in 2015.

Reflecting on what needs to be in place and what could stand in the way of successful adoption of whole-school thematic teaching, Hannah realized there were quite a few questions about how to prepare and introduce this new instructional strategy to both teachers and students. Based on her experience doing some theme work in her classroom this year, Hannah knows that many of her students will need some scaffolding in order to engage productively in more open-ended, project-based learning that requires them to make choices and follow their interests. Hannah explained:

> One thing that appeals to me about theme teaching is cultivating student passions. But it scares me how many of my students don't express any interests or passions. I have lots of kids who don't get excited about things. For example, they get to choose in writers' workshop what to write about. . . . I see that it's really hard for some kids because, for whatever reason, the natural curiosity you'd expect a kid to have is not present. I see it break down completely along SES and cultural lines. My two . . . middle-class students are both very passionate; they could talk your ear off about a lot of varied things because they clearly had lots of interests. They've been exposed to lots of different things, and they ask a lot of questions themselves.

Hannah's observation might confirm a general perception, that project-based learning is good for privileged students and that poor kids of color need more structure and skills-based instruction, but she strongly disagrees with this assessment. Hannah is committed to teaching in a way that provides all students with opportunities to develop and share their own ideas, strengths, and interests. She sees thematic units as a way to create such a culture within her classroom and the school as a whole. But she is also aware that she will need to find ways to scaffold for students who are not yet accustomed to or comfortable with making choices, sharing ideas, and so on.

Another potential obstacle that worries Hannah is the current lack of clarity around what is meant by *thematic teaching*. She has observed that teachers seem to have different ideas about what they'll be doing; some think it will just be a small part of their day, an overlay on top of their "regular" curriculum, while others understand it to be a more integral part of their planning process—integrating content across subjects within thematic units. Still others do not seem to have a good grasp on what thematic teaching might look like at all. Considering the nascent stage the school is in around their planning for this ambitious proposal, it's not surprising that there's a general lack of cohesion among staff. What worries Hannah is that no one at the school is in a position to offer the kind of framework that founding Mission Hill School staff had to work with in the beginning stages of its development.

CONCLUSION

There are multiple reasons why school leaders might decide to embark on the ambitious venture of enacting whole-school or schoolwide thematic teaching. Regardless of the reasoning, however, the more teachers are able to collaborate with one another, the richer and more sustainable the experience will be for all involved. From a leadership perspective, especially in the current climate of endless crises and reform, whole-school thematic units can be seen as one way to create a shared sense of purpose and vision among staff, one of the most important conditions underlying a strong and sustainable school culture, according to a long line of school-improvement scholars (see, for example, Anderson, 2009; Bryke, Sebring, Allensworth, Luppescu, & Easton, 2010; Fullan, 2007; Giles, 2007; Hargreaves & Goodson, 2006; Mourshed, Chijioke, & Barber, 2010). Whole-school themes, therefore, should be considered not only as a curriculum and instruction-enhancing mechanism but also as a way to embed structures and conditions conducive to sustainable school improvement. This was the knowledge that Meier brought to her vision for Mission Hill School, and it was my experience as a founding staff member that the school's mission was only as real or cohesive as it was in the collective commitment and daily practice of its staff.

The importance of creating strong collegial relationships through structured time for collaboration cannot be overstated. Thematic units invite teachers and students to take an active role in writing the narrative for their own learning. Now, nearly 2 decades after writing the pilot proposal, and 10 years after Meier has retired from her position as school principal, Mission Hill's schoolwide thematic teaching and the empowering democratic principles underlying them are still alive and strong. Working and planning together and being trusted to carry essential aspects of the school mission create that delicate balance between maintaining a cohesive culture while also avoiding the danger of stagnation.

In a sense, while schoolwide themes are a core element of Mission Hill School's organizational structure, they are not, in and of themselves, the most important aspect of the school culture. Rather, themes act as a vehicle that allows the school community to rally around common goals and values. This was highlighted at one staff retreat I observed as part of a research project I was conducting in 2009. At the end of every school year, the staff meets for several days to reflect on the past and plan for the year to come. One discussion I documented focused on revisiting "practices and cultural elements" that staff felt were central to the school's mission. The staff generated a long list that includes thematic units (which appears in the list below as *rotating themes and curriculum*) among many other important practices and values.

Essential Mission Hill Practices and Elements*

- Project-based learning
- Recess for all
- Access to art and the arts
- Portfolio assessment and narrative reports
- Cross-age grade experiences that are academic and social
- Large blocks of (work) time
- Experience-based learning/learning in and out of the classroom
- *Rotating themes and curriculum* [emphasis added]
- Safety and security
- Older students as role models
- Athletics
- Adult-student relationships

*Excerpted from a longer list generated by Mission Hill School staff, June 2009

I raise this as a way to emphasize that it is not the themes themselves that create cohesion, a culture of caring, or a model of democratic education. The fact that time has been set aside to revisit practices and elements that staff value most, that nothing is taken for granted or assumed to be set in stone, is what makes thematic teaching, and the school as a whole, successful. This is an important point to heed, especially for school leaders wishing to bring schoolwide themes into settings that already have established practices and cultural norms. At Mission Hill, common themes were seen from the beginning as a particularly promising structure to support the school's underlying pedagogical and philosophical missions. Without that underlying vision, asking teachers to work on common themes together risks becoming just another empty mandate. While no single strategy or practice will alleviate all the pressure and problems that schools face, this book advocates schoolwide themes as an important piece of the reform puzzle, one that, if done well, has the potential of helping schools create conditions that enrich student learning, sustain teachers' professional engagement, and greatly increase a sense of cohesion within the school as a whole.

NOTES

1. All names used in this chapter are pseudonyms to protect the identities of participants.

2. For many years, Mission Hill School was divided into two "houses," each composed of a set of K–5 classrooms. This was done to support our commitment to knowing every student well. While there were only 160 students in the school, we felt we could know them better and address professional concerns more efficiently if we were each primarily responsible for just 80 kindergarten to 5th-grade students. The middle school, 6–8th grade, met as a separate team.

3. I would like to thank all of the DC teachers who took time to participate in this study. Your reflections and wisdom were invaluable to completing this work.

REFERENCES

Anderson, S. E., & Kumari, R. (2009). Continuous improvement in schools: Understanding the practice. *International Journal of Educational Development, 29,* 281–292.

Bryke, A., Sebring, P. B., Allensworth, E., Luppescu, S., & Easton, J. Q. (2010). *Organizing schools for improvement: Lessons from Chicago.* Chicago, IL: University of Chicago Press.

Fullan, M. (2007). Educational reform as continuous improvement. In W. Hawley, & D. L. Rollie (Eds.), *The keys to effective schools: Educational reform as continuous improvement* (pp.1–9). Thousand Oaks, CA: Corwin Press.

Giles, C. (2007). Capacity building: Sustaining urban secondary schools as resilient self-renewing organizations in the face of standardized education reform. *The Urban Review, 40*(2), 137–163.

Hargreaves, A., & Goodson, I. (2006). Educational change over time? The sustainability of three decades of secondary change and continuity. *Educational Administration Quarterly, 42*(3), 3–41.

Mourshed, M., Chijioke, C., & Barber, M. (2010, November). *How the world's most improved school systems keep getting better.* London, England: McKinsey & Company.

CHAPTER 11

Conclusion

Deborah Meier
Matthew Knoester
Katherine Clunis D'Andrea

The Mission Hill School is a small, culturally diverse, democratically governed, K–8 public pilot school in the Boston Public Schools dedicated to education for democratic citizenship. The school uses portfolios of student work for assessment, and its graduates have been shown to achieve academic success in high school and college. Just as each teacher sought to create a classroom of strong, differentiated students—each of whom functioned as an independent and confident learner—he or she also sought to create a community of learners, and so too did the school aim for such a goal, schoolwide. The teachers at Mission Hill School have thought outside the box of traditional schooling, so the school has several unusual features as it works to address these questions.

One unique feature of the school is its approach to curriculum that involves whole-school 3-month thematic units. Each year, the entire school (with partial exception of the middle school) explores three broad thematic units together. These broad themes allow students to experience a sense of immersion in this "world of inquiry," and allow teachers and students to design and plan together smaller emergent inquiries in their own classrooms within these themes. The teachers at the school are able to share information and resources, including guest speakers, musicians, artifacts, fieldtrips, and books, as well as choose areas of inquiry that enable them to draw on their deep knowledge and interests, a crucial part of powerful education (Cochran-Smith & Zeichner, 2005; Darling-Hammond, 1997a, 1997b, 2010; Hargreaves & Fullan, 2012; Kumashiro, 2012) The power of aesthetics also plays a key role in this work. The faculty at the Mission Hill School believe that the aesthetic value of student work can have a transformational effect on the identities of students. For this reason, many of the projects and activities completed by students within long thematic units undergo multiple drafts, along with peer and adult critique within a noncompetitive and supportive environment.

Projects are designed by teachers and students to be eventually presentable before audiences of peers, parents, and members of the community. Some of the many ways that students present their work is through the whole-school gathering every Friday called Friday Share. Each gathering features presentations from students representing half the classes of the school, updating the rest of the school on what they are working on. Since the entire school is sharing an inquiry into the same broad theme, these gatherings have the effect of enriching all of the students' understanding about the theme and allow students a unique opportunity to develop public speaking and presentation skills (something that becomes highly necessary during the 7th- and 8th-grade portfolio presentations). Other ways students present their work is by showcasing their projects in the hallways and on classroom walls, presenting work at the bimonthly Family Nights (evenings during which parents gather to share food and view and learn about student work and learning), and offering individual class presentations and performances.

The curricular goals of the school are focused on developing habits of mind, the habits of asking, "From whose perspective is this told?" "What is the evidence for this assertion?" "Why should I care about this issue/why is it important?" "How is this connected to something else I know about?" and "Can I imagine how this might be different?" (in short: Viewpoint, Evidence, Relevance, Connections, and Conjecture). The mark of a good curriculum is that there are many opportunities to practice these habits of mind. By organizing the curriculum of the school around three yearly schoolwide themes, we have been able to explore big ideas, with many opportunities for students to see connections, imagine new worlds, and explore evidence from multiple viewpoints.

To recap, this book has provided detail into how children and adults go about this work, with each chapter written by a different teacher or administrator who has been part of carrying out these tasks, focusing on a particular theme or aspect of this work.

After the history and rationales for this work were introduced in the opening chapters, in Chapters 3 and 4 teachers Katherine Clunis D'Andrea and Geralyn Bywater McLaughlin, respectively, described particular themes within their early childhood classrooms, focusing on the units called "The World of Work" and "Natural Science." Clunis D'Andrea richly described how she and her students created an in-depth inquiry into bakeries and transformed their classroom into a bakery that served the entire school community. Bywater McLaughlin described her work with the subtheme "Garden Friends," part of the "Natural Science" theme, and illustrated how students interacting with and inquiring into living plants and animals can allow students to grow in so many academic and social ways, as students are also often thinking about the media-driven materialistic influences, as evidenced by obsessions with clothes and particular name brands.

Chapter 5, by Jenerra Williams, and Chapter 6, by Matthew Knoester, richly described thematic units in middle childhood grades, focusing on the themes "The Struggle for Justice" and "Physical Science," respectively. In these chapters, the authors illustrated how they focused on aspects to be discerned within the broader schoolwide themes. Williams focused on the civil rights movement, in the whole-school theme of "The Struggle for Justice: U.S. History Through the Eyes of African Americans," through the lens of photography and poetry, bringing out intense engagement with these media and this subject matter with her students. Knoester described his students' exploration of astronomy within the "Physical Science" theme. This theme included real-time moon- and stargazing, as well as research on the history of astronomical ideas over the past several thousand years, culminating with a "space museum," where students showcased their work for an audience of other students, teachers, and parents in the school.

Chapter 7 described the unique approach of art teacher Jeanne Rachko, as she explained her role as the primary point person for the art room at the school. Using the whole-school thematic unit of "Ancient China" as an example, Rachko described how she organizes the art room and her own schedule to work with each classroom once a week, as well as allows small groups of students to "drop in" to the art room studio space for large chunks of time throughout the week. Additionally, she serves as a consultant to all the teachers in the school as they include art in their explorations of the whole-school themes and showcase the students' work throughout the school.

In Chapter 8, former middle school and 2nd- and 3rd-grade teacher Heidi Lyne described assessment at Mission Hill School, paying particular focus to the robust portfolios that are required for graduation from the school. As one of the founding teachers of the school, Lyne helped to design the portfolio process at Mission Hill School, and she notes how the performance assessment approach of the school—much more so than traditional standardized tests—is an excellent example of the robust new forms of assessment that are being demanded by various regulatory authorities, and she makes an argument for performance assessments, such as portfolios, as the most appropriate set of tools for understanding students' learning in various disciplines.

In Chapter 9, the current principal of the school, Ayla Gavins, described special education and professional development at the school, with particular focus on the recent surge in students with special needs at the school. The entire school needed to rethink its approach to effectively including students of all abilities in the classroom, and Gavins described the culture of critical reflection and mutual learning among adults in the school, including teacher inquiry and descriptive reviews of student work.

Chapter 10, written by founding teacher Emily Gasoi, began with examples of her 2nd- and 3rd-grade unit on ancient Egypt, but she continued to describe how she gathered research from graduates of the Mission Hill School as she completed her EdD thesis from the University of Pennsylvania. During and following the time of her research, she also served as a coach to other teachers in various schools in the Washington, DC, area. She described how teachers working in various settings think and work with many of the themes raised in this book. Gasoi pointed out the fact that many of the teachers she worked with wished to implement the basic features of deep and rich thematic units, like those described in this book, but also found significant constraints to do so, based on the school cultures in which they worked. Nevertheless, Gasoi argued that it is possible and desirable to learn from the crucial work of the Mission Hill School, and problems of collaboration, student engagement, and differentiation can and must be addressed, regardless of school location. Despite the current focus on standardized learning in education today, it is also notable that there has been a mini-boom in literature focusing on broad thematic learning in classrooms, with clear examples of teachers carrying out this work (Bender, 2012; Berger, 2003; Egan, 2011, 2014; Helm, 2010, 2015; Krauss & Boss, 2013).

Unfortunately, there are many other aspects of the school, and of this approach to whole-school learning, that we were not able to present in this book. For example, after reading these chapters, it may be hard to imagine what one thematic unit looks like across all the grades as they are implemented simultaneously, but also differently for children of various ages.

The study of natural science and monarch butterflies, for instance, might involve a great deal of observing, measuring, reading, and making art in an early childhood classroom, while in an upper-level classroom, students might be studying the paths of monarch migration, conducting closer observation with the use of microscopes, studying the life cycles of monarchs, reading and writing books with much more content about insects and specific features of monarchs, and so on.

Another aspect of the school that is impossible to fully appreciate after reading the chapters of this book are the ways in which the parents of students are deeply involved with this work. For example, parents are invited to—and many of them regularly attend—the weekly Friday Share whole-school gatherings, where students sing and present their works in progress. Family members regularly attend bimonthly Family Nights, where food is shared and student work is presented for those who cannot make it to Friday Shares. Families are invited to many of the staff planning meetings. Families have their own Family Council that regularly meets and discusses important aspects of the school. Out of the Family Council, several representatives are elected to sit on the school's governance board, which makes critical decisions, such as the hiring and evaluation of the principal and passing a budget. Families are expected to attend two formal conferences with their child's teacher each year, and there are many documents sent home to families, including the weekly newsletter and two formal report cards or narrative reports. This is all in addition to any informal communication between families and their child's teacher. Each of these forms of communication and participation deserves much more elaboration, as parent participation and governance are a critical part of the school, but at this point, we must point the reader to other books written about the school that provide a more robust description of these aspects of the school (Knoester, 2012a; Meier, 2002; Meier, Sizer, & Sizer, 2004).

This book has included positive examples of how the curriculum of the school is designed and how the work is carried out, but much more could be said about the current climate of education policy, which is dominated by high-stakes standardized tests. This policy climate has negatively affected the work described in this book in countless ways, discussion of which is beyond the scope of this book. Again, we will have to point the reader to other publications that have argued from this standpoint (Knoester, 2011, 2012a; Meier, 2000, 2002; Meier & Wood, 2004; Nichols & Berliner, 2007).

This book has also left out the basic statistics of the school, including student demographics, test scores, graduation rates, college-going rates, attendance rates, and behavior incidences. These statistics are gathered and analyzed in various places (Boston Public Schools, 2014; Center for Collaborative Education, 2006; Gasoi, 2012; Knoester, 2012a, 2012b; Massachusetts Department of Elementary and Secondary Education, 2014). In short, the graduates of the Mission Hill School do very well upon graduation. They generally attend high schools of their choice (including selective private and public high schools) and pass the 10th-grade state graduation exam, and 96% of college-age graduates have entered college. However, the standardized test scores of the Mission Hill School student body are mixed. The school's averages in both language arts and math at all levels tested are above the averages for the Boston Public Schools but below state averages, consistent with the findings of various scholars who have shown the close correlation between standardized test scores and socioeconomic status (Nichols & Berliner, 2007). This book has also left out the particular contexts that have allowed this school to make decisions about its curriculum, governance structure, budget, hiring practices, and schedule. As a pilot school within the Boston Public Schools, it is given relative autonomy in these areas, and the school has made decisions that are quite unique in the Boston Public Schools, and elsewhere. More information about the politics and particular agreements among stakeholders in Boston that enable these decisions can be found elsewhere (see Center for Collaborative Education, 2006; Knoester, 2011, 2012a; Meier, 2002; Meier, Sizer & Sizer, 2004).

In the end, what we hope readers will take away from this book are that students and schools can be more powerful places of learning if they break down the barriers to fruitful collaboration that is possible within their walls. We have illustrated how this small school has organized itself to reach a high level of collaboration and shared learning across nine grade levels and a wide spectrum of abilities. Chapter authors have richly described how they have designed and carried out powerful and enriching thematic units that have brought out creativity and decisionmaking on the parts of students and created opportunities for students to develop unique inquiries around their genuine interests. Authors also point to resources and ideas used to create this culture of immersion and and how they have encouraged critical thinking about big ideas. Throughout all the age levels, teachers and students draw on the five habits of mind that frame the curricular goals of the school: the habits of asking, "What is the evidence?" "How is this connected to what I already know?" "How could this turn out differently?" "From whose perspective is this coming?" and "What is the relevance of this question; why should I care?" Based on surveys and interviews with graduates, we know that the experiences students have at the school create meaningful connections and become lasting memories that they take with them, well beyond the walls of Mission Hill School.

REFERENCES

Bender, W. N. (2012). *Project-based learning: Differentiating instruction for the 21st century.* Newbury Park, CA: Corwin.

Berger, R. (2003). *An ethic of excellence: Building a culture of craftsmanship with students.* Portsmouth, NH: Heinemann.

Boston Public Schools. (2014). Mission Hill K–8 School. Retrieved from www.bostonpublicschools.org/school/mission-hill-k-8-school

Center for Collaborative Education. (2006). *Progress and promise: Results from the Boston pilot schools.* Boston, MA: Author.

Cochran-Smith, M., & Zeichner, K. (2005). *Studying teacher education: The report of the AERA panel on research and teacher education.* New York, NY: Lawrence Earlbaum.

Darling-Hammond, L. (1997a). *The right to learn: A blueprint for creating schools that work.* San Francisco, CA: Jossey-Bass.

Darling-Hammond, L. (1997b). *Doing what matters most: Investing in quality teaching.* New York, NY: National Commission on Teaching and America's Future.

Darling-Hammond, L. (2010). *The flat world and education: How America's commitment to equity will determine our future.* New York, NY: Teachers College Press.

Egan, K. (2011). *Learning in depth: A simple innovation that can transform schooling.* Chicago, IL: The University of Chicago Press.

Egan, K. (2014). *Whole-school projects: Engaging imaginations through interdisciplinary inquiry.* New York, NY: Teachers College Press.

Gasoi, E. (2012). *Active accountability: A cross-case study of two schools negotiating improvement, change, and organizational integrity.* Unpublished doctoral dissertation, University of Pennsylvania, Philadelphia, PA.

Hargreaves, A., & Fullan, M. (2012). *Professional capital: Transforming teaching in every school.* New York, NY: Teachers College Press.

Helm, J. H. (2010). *Young investigators: The project approach in the early years* (2nd ed.). New York, NY: Teachers College Press.

Helm, J. H. (2015). *Becoming young thinkers: Deep project work in the classroom.* New York, NY: Teachers College Press.

Knoester, M. (2011). Is the outcry for more pilot schools warranted? Democracy, collective bargaining, deregulation, and the politics of school reform in Boston. *Educational Policy, 25*(3), 387–423.

Knoester, M. (2012a). *Democratic education in practice: Inside the Mission Hill School.* New York, NY: Teachers College Press.

Knoester, M. (2012b). *International struggles for critical democratic education.* New York, NY: Peter Lang.

Krauss, J. I., & Boss, S. K. (2013). *Thinking through project-based learning: Guiding deeper inquiry.* Newbury Park, CA: Corwin.

Kumashiro, K. K. (2012). *Bad teacher! How blaming teachers distorts the bigger picture.* New York, NY: Teachers College Press.

Massachusetts Department of Elementary and Secondary Education. (2014). *School and district profiles: MA Department of Elementary and Secondary Education.* Retrieved from profiles.doe.mass.edu/profiles/general.aspx?topNavId=1&org code=00350382&orgtypecode=6&

Meier, D. W. (2000). *Will standards save public education?* Boston, MA: Beacon Press.

Meier, D. W. (2002). *In schools we trust: Creating communities of learning in an era of testing and standardization.* Boston, MA: Beacon Press.

Meier, D. W., Sizer, T. R., & Sizer, N. F. (2004). *Keeping school: Letters to families from principals of two small schools.* Boston, MA: Beacon Press.

Meier, D. W., & Wood, G. (Eds.). (2004). *Many children left behind: How the No Child Left Behind Act is damaging our children and our schools.* Boston, MA: Beacon Press.

Nichols, S. L., & Berliner, D. C. (2007). *Collateral damage: How high-stakes testing corrupts America's schools.* Cambridge, MA: Harvard Education Press.

Afterword

Filming *A Year at Mission Hill*

Tom Valens and Amy Valens

In the fall of 2008 I (Amy) wrote a letter to an author I admired, wondering if she might be willing to look at footage my husband and I had selected from what he had filmed during my last year of teaching. I had read Deborah Meier's *The Power of Their Ideas* and hoped she would be interested in helping us sort out what was most important to tell in the film that we had titled *AUGUST TO JUNE: Bringing Life to School*.

Along with her very valuable comments on the 40-minute assembly we sent her came the wistful remark "I wish wish wish it had also focused on a school that had a lot of kids of color." This was the seed that led to a call to principal Ayla Gavins soon after *August to June* premiered in January 2011, to see if the progressive school Deborah Meier had founded in Boston would be willing to have the intrusion of filmmakers documenting what they were doing. By August that same year we were a two-person team observing and recording Mission Hill's before-school retreat.

It is not unusual for teachers to meet for a day or two before school, but we were not prepared for the intensity, honesty, and enthusiasm of this total-immersion retreat. It was open to all staff members and almost all were there: 10 lead teachers; 3 paraprofessionals; aftercare staff; speech, occupational therapy, reading, and art specialists; student teachers; interns; the principal; and more.

Wanting to make sure people were comfortable with us, much to our regret we missed documenting the powerful process of the first morning, when the staff reviewed the school's mission statement and expressed what that meant to each of them personally and in relation to how they taught. By that afternoon, as in small groups they shared how they intended to approach the first all-school theme, we had the camera rolling and were wishing we could be everywhere at once. Each conversation was a rich time for ideas to be thoughtfully explored, excitement shared, questions asked, and suggestions considered. If we hadn't heard people introduce themselves, we wouldn't have known who was a lead teacher and who had some other position on staff from the way they participated in the discussions. Everyone seemed equally engaged and respected. Wow.

We live in California and would not be able to spend as much time at school as Tom had spent in my classroom, so we were looking for how to space our visits. That first afternoon we realized that the three schoolwide themes would help us tell the story. We would time our visits to catch the unfolding of each.

The first one, "Natural Sciences," was the subject of discussion as we filmed the retreat. This very wide-open topic prompted the most diverse responses, with curriculum being developed around insects (butterflies and bees), trees, ecosystems, life cycles, energy, and the human body. One teacher talked about all the ways she could integrate art, math, and literature into the theme; two others discussed how older students could work with younger ones. Another admitted that he had not felt success-ful the last time he presented this theme. He wanted to be more concrete this time around and was soliciting ideas from his colleagues. Still another listened eagerly to his student intern, whose background would bring ad-ditional resources into the classroom. Everyone's plans were open ended, with room for what their students would add.

Jenerra's sharing at the retreat was typical. She was going to do a unit on bees. She started by describing all the things she was excited about and the materials she had gathered. She had had a demonstration hive in her classroom for years but was still thinking about how to best use it with her 2nd- and 3rd-graders. Following an agreed-upon protocol, the group engaged in several stages of questioning, at first just asking for clarification of her intentions and then broadening to people's thoughts about children studying bees. The fear of insects and bee stings was brought up (perhaps a way to discuss irrational and rational fears?), as was the social structure of bees as it compares to our own. Had she figured a budget for her field trips? There was a point where Jenerra's role was to listen and take notes while others threw her ideas around. The session ended with Jenerra's reflections and where they led her.

Back in the classrooms, we watched how the reactions of students built and transformed their teacher's plans. The platform that Jacob's 8th-graders built to help the younger students observe the beehive became a favorite spot not just for observing the hive but also as a special perch for journal writing. Tato beamed with initiative as he bounced over to Jeanne's art room to borrow a book on butterflies, bringing it back and discussing his findings with his friends. Then there was the story that Jada's kinder-garten/ 1st-grade class published in the school newsletter (dictated to Jada by her students):

Caterpillar Disappearance and the Little Caterpillar

Once upon a time there was a little caterpillar. When it was small it was tiny. It ate a lot and it grew a lot. It ate lots and lots and lots of milkweed. It had 16 legs and it pooped a lot. We saw the fat caterpillar and a big caterpillar. One day one of our caterpillars drowned into the water and there was only one left. The other caterpillar climbed and climbed and climbed like Jack and Annie in the Magic Tree House. It hung in a j for a long time. We thought that it would turn into a chrysalis, a cocoon or a pupa. Then it would pop open and out would come a butterfly!

But that did not happen. One morning the caterpillar was gooey on its head. The caterpillar almost turned into a butterfly. Then there was a mouse inside the container. The caterpillar disappeared and the caterpillar turned into a mouse! But caterpillars don't turn into mice because if that was true then that would be crazy and we would know. We know that caterpillars really turn into butterflies. So, it must be that the mouse got in and then it ate the caterpillar. We don't know how the mouse got in.

As was often the case with Jada's submissions to the newsletter, after she quoted her students, she added where she would take their ideas:

Due to this very hungry mouse, we continue to review the correct stages in this life cycle. However, what do you do when your mind tells you one thing but your eyes tell you another?

Jada's answer was to take her class to the butterfly garden at the Museum of Science where they witnessed a real butterfly emerge from a chrysalis, and spread its wings.

Amy had taught thematically for years, and many teachers do, but here was a whole staff making a single topic the focus of in-depth learning across all areas of study for long periods of time. We experienced the richness that comes when the commitment of the entire school is so complete.

We filmed during two of the themes that are discussed in this book. In each case one of the pieces that we appreciated was the overlap between the content and the ongoing work teachers were doing to support the growth of individual students socially, emotionally, and intellectually.

When we arrived for our midyear shoot, the Chinese dragons that the oldest students had made were already covering the hallway walls. Creating something both intricate and whimsical was just the right challenge for middle schoolers. The younger students studied those dragons, pointing out details, when making their way up and down the hallway. It was not unusual to see an older child pointing out the piece he or she had worked on to a younger schoolmate. Clearly the oldest students' engagement had a positive influence on the whole school.

The theme of "Ancient China" lent itself to many different art experiences, with much collaboration between Jeanne in the art room and teachers in their classrooms. Jeanne had mentioned at the beginning-of-the-year retreat that she intended to thread a variety of ways to use inks into the art experiences she designed. Brushstroke calligraphy was a natural for the Chinese theme, and we were lucky enough to be there the day a Chinese student from Harvard came by to demonstrate. While Kathy's kindergarten and 1st-grade students worked with brushes and ink, Jeanne not only encouraged them as artists but also found opportunities to reinforce the habits of mind so important to the pedagogy of the school. Jovanni, often an impatient and easily frustrated young person, was very satisfied with what he was producing. So he said out loud, "This is easy for me!" Jolie, who was sitting at the same table with him, told him that he shouldn't say that because "it might be hard for someone else"—meaning it wasn't easy for her. Jeanne's response was respectful of both children. She asked Jolie in an empathetic voice if it was hard for her, and she modeled for Jovanni a way to listen to another person's perspective. A short while later Jovanni worried that Alejandro was copying him. Jeanne's reply then is one I wish every art teacher would remember: "We take inspiration from everything that's around us, so if he is looking at your work, that means he's inspired by what you are doing, and that's how we learn."

Jeanne balanced the focused work of imitating the Chinese words with plenty of free exploration of brushes and ink. Abstract designs, flowers, and geometric patterns flowed from the happily absorbed children, and every student was treated as an individual finding his or her own way with the material, including Jhayden, who happily filled his entire sheet until it was solid black.

Mission Hill is a full-inclusion school, and over and over we watched the integration of children with special needs. Jhayden loved the art room, coming more often to engage in experiential play with the dolls and animals and dress-up clothes that Jeanne kept there than to create a finished product. That was true of the way he used the ink as well. Even though Jeanne was not a classroom teacher, she participated, along with other staff and specialists, in a variety of small-group meetings where the needs of a particular child were discussed. She had the background to see that Jhayden was getting what he needed from the brush-and-ink experience as much as the child who painted a flower with elegant simplicity, more reminiscent of Chinese art.

Hamdi was a delightful child diagnosed with Down syndrome and being fully included. We watched her painting her Chinese mask. Her classmates easily included her, helping her matter-of-factly only when needed. Every child in the school had the opportunity to make a mask, so we were able to see how the same project evolved as children of different ages and abilities attacked it. Jeanne set the mood with music, but had to turn it off when we shot, so that we would be able to intercut scenes when we edited. She made that concession graciously, but we knew how important that element was to ambiance in the room. When we weren't filming, we enjoyed watching how students moved in rhythm with what she played.

Many of the oldest students remembered sitting still while a plaster cast of their face was made at least once before, as Jeanne had brought that project to the art room other times. This time each of them would be the person applying the plaster to a classmate, then taking a turn with the roles reversed. So many layers of learning were going on! Typical adolescent self-consciousness had to be tossed aside as your partner smoothed wet plaster cloth over your face, making sure to keep an air passage open! The thinking that was behind their color and design choices became clear to us months later, when we listened to 7th- and 8th-graders describe this project as part of their portfolio assessment.

The next time we returned the school had moved on to their final theme, "The World of Work," and Kathy's students were rolling out pastry dough. Flops were part of the process, and pies didn't make it to the menu at the bakery, but the strawberry jam we watched them canning did. Kadian was very impressed with an odd-looking tool that Kathy had placed together with the canning jars. No amount of explaining could have taught him as well as letting him manipulate it. He squealed with pleasure when he figured out that these were tongs specially designed to lift jars in and out of the hot water. And speaking of hot water, there was plenty of hot water in the canning pot. Even though there were children in that classroom at an early point in learning to control their impulses, it was clear that they were proud of the trust Kathy had in them that they could handle a potentially dangerous situation. They all used appropriate caution when they were near the canner. When people talk about having high expectations that students rise to, we think of this example as a very concrete one, leavened with the fact that it was the end of the school year, and Kathy had built many experiences for these children so they were ready for the responsibility she gave them.

Bringing together resources that widen the children's perspective was a big part of this project. We missed Kathy's visit to West End bakeries but were there for all the steps involved in making strawberry jam, including writing a book and designing a label for their product. For the label they were in contact via the Internet with a graphic designer. He was going to take their idea and create a finished product that could be duplicated. Kathy made a list of student suggestions for what were important elements of a label, and then those who wanted to submitted designs for the logo. Zayna's parachuting snail was what the children thought best met their criteria. Kathy scanned the image so the graphic artist could work in collaboration with her students. He sent them several versions of how he could use her drawing. The students crowded around the computer discussing what he had produced, in much the same way they had discussed their own contributions, and giving feedback. They were already getting accustomed to the idea that it takes time and revisions before a final product is reached.

Having been at school filming on three other occasions for a total of 8 weeks, we knew many of Kathy's students quite well by the time they were ready to open the Parachuting Snail Bakery. Here is what one shift of the bakery looked like, from the perspective of how the work of the theme complemented the social and emotional growth each child was making: Irea, who Kathy once described as her firecracker, was calmly surveying the baskets of baked goods, crossing off her inventory sheet, and remembering to tell people very sweetly, "Do come again!" Kadian, who on the first day of school couldn't stop crying, and couldn't verbalize what was wrong, was clearly explaining the ingredients in each baked good. Jhayden, who a few months ago rarely made eye contact and might suddenly run and hide, was urging people to tell him what they wanted to buy. True, he also ate some of the merchandise. But when confronted he stuck around and apologized. At the cash box was shy Cyrus. His doing math in his head and making change was no surprise, but confidently handing the change to his customers was a new skill. Had they learned about the world of work? Yes. But even more important, they had tasted the pleasure of seeing their ideas realized and of going from questions to actions that gave them answers and expertise.

The school year ended and we set to work, first making a 10-part Internet series, 3 of which were completely devoted to the three themes of the year. One of the goals of the series was to cross-pollinate ideas between a group of close to 50 organizations involved in work related to progressive education. Each episode of the series would run on the websites or be commented on by groups from the Ashoka Institute and CASEL, who focus on empathy and social emotional learning, to Fairtest, whose focus is developing better ways to assess growth than standardized tests, along with the American Federation of Teachers, Edutopia, *Yes* magazine, and many more. Sam Chaltain created a Prezi that grew as each episode was posted, and the staff at IDEA (the Institute for Democratic Education in America) kept adding backup material to the series website. The Prezi has been seen over 217,300 times. As of April 2015, the YouTube channel had a total of over 75,000 views. IDEA estimated that by November 2013 over 100,000 people had viewed some or all of the series at public and private screenings. Chapters are being used for university courses, for professional development workshops, at education conferences, and by individuals. We see that the positive image of a school where teachers are able to build curriculum that has meaning for them and their students, and where children's ideas are valued, is a powerful motivator for parents and teachers.

The final piece of our part in this endeavor is the one-hour film *Good Morning Mission Hill: The Freedom to Teach, the Freedom to Learn*, which began playing on public television stations across the nation in August 2014. With it we hope to convince people who might not have spent time in schools recently of the tremendous learning energy released when teachers and students have the freedom to dive together into subjects that fascinate the eyes, the ears, the hands, the heart, and the mind. This book's further elaboration of thematic teaching will be invaluable as the place to go next to understand in more depth the inner workings of that process.

Access to the video series, *A Year at Mission Hill*, as well as more information about the film, *Good Morning Mission Hill*, can be found at www.goodmorningmissionhill.com

Mission Hill School Sequence of Themes, Habits of Mind, and Mission Statement

The Sequence of Whole-School Thematic Units at the Mission Hill School

	Fall	Winter	Spring
Year 1	U.S. History/Current Events: Whose Voice Counts? (Government and Elections)	Ancient Greece	Physical Science
Year 2	Natural Science	Ancient Maya/Taino	U.S. History/Current Events: The World of Work
Year 3	U.S. History/Current Events: The Struggle for Justice Through the Eyes of African Americans	Ancient Egypt	Physical Science
Year 4	Natural Science	Ancient China	U.S. History/Current Events: Who Are We? Where Did We Come From? (Immigration/Migration)

Mission Hill School Habits of Mind

Evidence: How do you know, and how certain are you?

Viewpoint: From whose perspective is this coming? Might we understand it differently from another perspective?

Connections: How is this connected to what we already know? Is there a pattern?

Relevance: Why is this important?

Conjecture: How could this be different from what it is? Can we imagine a different past, present, or future?

Mission Hill School Mission Statement

The task of public education is to help parents raise youngsters who will maintain and nurture the best habits of a democratic society: be smart, caring, strong, resilient, imaginative and thoughtful. It aims at producing youngsters who can live productive, socially useful and personally satisfying lives, while also respecting the rights of all others. The school, as we see it, will help strengthen our commitment to diversity, equity and mutual respect.

Democracy requires citizens with the capacity to step into the shoes of others, even those we most dislike, to sift and weigh alternatives, to listen respectfully to other viewpoints with the possibility in mind that we each have something to learn from others. It requires us to be prepared to defend intelligently that which we believe to be true, and that which we believe best meets our individual needs and those of our family, community and broader public—to not be easily conned. It requires also the skills and competencies to be well informed and persuasive—to read well, to write and speak effectively and persuasively, and to handle numbers and calculations with competence and confidence.

Democracy requires citizens who are themselves artists and inventors—knowledgeable about the accomplishments, performances, products and inventions of others but also capable of producing, performing and inventing their own art. Without art we are all deprived.

Such habits of mind, and such competence, are sustained by our enthusiasms, as well as our love for others and our respect for ourselves, and our willingness to persevere, deal with frustration and develop reliable habits of work. Our mission is to create a community in which our children and their families can best maintain and nurture such democratic habits.

Toward these ends, our community must be prepared to spend time even when it might seem wasteful hearing each other out. We must deal with each other in ways that lead us to feel stronger and more loved, not weaker and less loveable. We must expect the most from everyone, hold all to the highest standards, but also respect our different ways of exhibiting excellence. We must together build a reasonable set of standards for our graduates so that they can demonstrate to us their capacity to meet this mission.

Sample Mission Hill School Newsletter

Este boletín está disponible en línea en español y otros idiomas. Ir a
www.missionhillschool.org/resources/newsletters/

VOLUME 17, ISSUE 19   FEBRUARY 7, 2014

Mission Hill School News

Letter from Child Street

Preparing for the Next Growing Season

Dear Mission Hill School Families, Friends, Students and Staff,

Moments after I ordered seedlings for my garden this past weekend, I wrote to a parent about her daughter's high school admissions. The actions—both related to preparing now for warmer days—came together.

In January and February it's time to plan many different "gardens". Daffodil bulbs were planted in our schoolyard at the same time that our 8th grade students applied to high schools. We will find out the results of both when the days are longer and warmer. Our school budget and staffing template for next year was due at the same time as a new order of honeybees for my hive. Grade 6 students will begin preparing now for spring Recollections, and summer camp applications will be due soon.

As students across the city find out about school assignments and we receive our new student roster, gardeners will be turning over soil and laying down new mulch for a hearty growing season. In the thick of New England winter, planning for sunnier days can be spirit lifting.

Below are few things happening now (and soon) at Mission Hill to keep in mind so we can have a more satisfying spring and summer:

• Camp Night at Mission Hill on Thursday, February 27 from 4 to 6 pm. Representatives from our partnering camps will be present with applications and information to help you find the right match for your child(ren).

• Family Conferences just ended. Keep the teacher comments from your child's progress report and family conference handy so your child doesn't forget what the goals are. The next report comes home at the end of March (just around the corner).

• Family Council meets on March 13 to discuss several action-oriented items. Please attend. Your voice and hands are needed to make the work ahead lighter. Tasks include planning for spring events and next year.

• The next Governance Board meeting is on Thursday, April 4. Attend for the most detailed information about school plans for next year.

• The Boston Public school calendar has been updated. Due to snow days, our new last day of school is June 24 if no more days are lost to cancellations.

I know you've got your personal lists too. Happy Planning !

~Ayla Gavins

REMINDERS

February
2/14: School Closed for staff conference
2/17-21: Winter break
2/26: Grades 3-6 to BSO concert - *Chaperones needed!*
2/27, 4:00 - 6:00: Camp Information Night
2/27, 6:00: Outside the Lines Mtg.

March
3/6, 5:00: Governance Board mtg.
3/13, 5:45: Family Council Mtg.
3/17: No School

VOLUME 17, ISSUE 19   FEBRUARY 7, 2014

From the Classrooms

3 and 4 year-olds

Room 108

As the entire school studies the Taíno people, our focus will be "The Nature of the Taíno". The Taíno believed that if you take care of the earth, the earth will take care of you. It is a natural connection to our fall study of learning how to take care of our animals, plants and each other. We have started our study of the Taíno by learning about the coquí. The coquí is a small frog that is famous for the loud song it sings at night. It is one of the most common frogs in Puerto Rico and it is about the same size as the garden snails we have in our classroom. Many thanks to Jada Brown for teaching us *El Coquí* , the children's song. Ask your child to sing it to you. (In our class we have a number of families with roots in Puerto Rico, so maybe you know the song already!)

~**Geralyn Bywater McLaughlin & Donna Winder**

Kindergarten

Room 106

For the past couple weeks we have been learning about the Taíno. Our research has turned into the building of a Taíno village in the block area. The children started by recreating the Taíno houses they had seen in books. They are circular and were challenging to build with blocks. They collaborated to figure out

the structure and how to add a room.

From our research we learned that the Taíno in Puerto Rico say beaches, mountains, rivers, and oceans (as well as other area). The students started to recreate those as well. They painted an ocean and added sea life. They painted a waterfall and created a pool and rocks at the base. They also painted a fruit tree.

One day James asked, "I want to make a fire, did the Taínos have fire?" I told him that they did. He then used blocks to create a circular shape. He tore yellow and red paper to create a fire effect. Come visit our Taíno village.

~**Kathy Clunis D'Andrea**

Room 107

While the excitement around the Taíno is growing, last week we took a small break from researching and constructing our large tree (complete with the coquí tree frogs we love so much). With the information we have already gathered, we wanted students to now think about what they would want to find out next.

Here are a few of their questions that will shape our study in the coming weeks:

"I wanna know if the Tainos were one of the first people to live on the world."

"What did the Tainos wear? Do the Tainos still live in Puerto Rico today?"

"Were they the first people to grow up? Do the Tainos do yoga?"

"Why doesn't the Taíno live in Boston? Where do they live?"

"Why do coquís say ribbit and their bellies get big? How long is the coquí's tongue?"

"Why do they have stones? How many hairs do they have? How long is their hair?"

"Why do they have animals? Do the Taínos eat meatballs?"

"How old are the Taínos? Who was older? Did the Taíno put water for ice?"

"Were their houses made of sticks?"

"Where do the Taino live in the earth so far away?"

"Where did the Taínos live? It's kind of hard to think in my head. And what do the Taínos eat? What did they build? Maybe their

Volume 17, Issue 19   February 7, 2014

house is made of wood and there is grass on the roof, and windows?"

"How does the coquí get big?"

"Do the Taíno eat chicken, rice, salad and spaghetti and meatballs? Do the Taínos drum?"

"Do they love to play and eat spaghetti and meatballs and turkey and chicken and hamburger?"

"I think they have pots."

"Where do the Taínos make plants?"

~**Jada Brown & JoAnn Hawksworth**

Room 109

Hello Mission Hill! The past two weeks the Original Stars have been learning more about the environment and climate of where the Taíno people lived. We have been talking about the rainforest, and what animals are found there. We discussed how these are animals the Taíno people may have seen, and we might be able to see if we went to the Caribbean Islands today. Each student has chosen a particular animal to focus on, and is creating his or her own information booklet. In their books, they can write facts, draw pictures, and pose questions about their rainforest animal.

This week was also family conferences. I hope all of you enjoyed the personalized tour lead by your children!

~**Liz Borson**

Grades One & Two

Room 204

No news this week

Room 205

Family conference time is so much more than just preparing for a conversation between families and teachers, especially the way conferences happen at Mission Hill. It is a time for families to see school and learning from their child's perspective. It teaches students to be reflective about their work and time spent at school. It allows teachers to learn even more about their students. What do they think is hard for them? What have they enjoyed working on? Where do they like to work best? We are with them all day long and have the opportunity to notice what we think are the answers to these questions and many others, but maybe our perceptions are wrong. We spent some time the past two weeks preparing for family visits. The students were given prompts to think about their experience at school and then they practiced sharing their reflections and tour of the classroom with their peers and teachers. Thank you so much for taking the time to come visit us at school. It is a very meaningful part of your child's learning.

~**Ashleigh L'Heureux**

Room 217

Recently we have had two guests in our classroom – they have brought their talents and expertise to the classroom to help us develop a richer understanding of the Taíno. Rob, Cyrus and Jasper's father and an oceanographer, designed an engaging presentation on oceans, with a particular focus on the relationship the Taíno had with the oceans. We now have an ocean mural in our classroom where we designed fish to show what we learned from his presentation.

Last week, Maria, a member of the custodial staff who is from Puerto Rico, prepared many vegetables (yucca, sweet potato, corn) and fruits (pineapples, guavas). We had an extensive Taíno Taste Test!

During both presentations, the students brought the Mission Hill habits of mind to life. They asked questions to gather evidence about the Taino. They made connections between our lives and the lives of people who lived long ago. They developed a sense of relevance about this topic.

~**Emma Fialka-Feldman**

Grades Three & Four

Room 207

This past week the Role Model Hawks have been preparing themselves for the annual family conferences. Students have taken the time to reflect on various aspects of their learning experiences within the Mission Hill walls. To help guide the wonderful classroom tours that took place this past Thursday and Friday students used a form we call the learning record. The learning record contains the following questions: (1) which area do you like best to work at inside of the classroom?, (2) what is something you are working on now?, (3) What is something you feel great about?, and (4) what is

VOLUME 17, ISSUE 19   FEBRUARY 7, 2014

something that is challenging you?

These questions are designed to give families and friends a snapshot of all of their experiences at school.

Their various types of art work, writing pieces, math work, and theme studies work is showcased around the classroom to provide evidence and support their remarks on the learning record and meeting with the teacher. It is always exciting to meet and discuss my students with all of you. I am excited to continue our work together throughout the remaining months of the school year. If there are any questions, comments, or concerns that were not shared at the conference please feel free to contact me directly.

~Robert Baez

Room 216

Greetings from Room 216, This past week we have been working on what life is like now and in the past, as well as figuring out their roles. Next week, we plan to take trip to the library to find more books on the Taíno. We have been reading a lot of books and researching online, trying to become experts in language, instruments, huts, hunting tools, theater performance, arts and crafts, cooking, and fishing.

We are beginning to find lots of interesting facts, such as what happened to the Taíno and why their history unfolded the way it did. The students have completed their Taíno maps and

they have started creating small dolls and clay huts.

Next week we hope to have a few wonderful guests come in and cook for us! Maria is an amazing cook and works within our school. She has already helped Emma's class with cooking using Taíno ingredients. We also have a wonderful parent in our class who is an amazing cook as well. The students will get a double dose of helping prepare a meal and eating the tasty results.

~Josh Kraus

Grades Five & Six

Room 210
No news this week

Room 215
No news this week

z

Grades Seven & Eight

Room 213

Over the years, I've been fortunate to be able to travel with students to participate in educational conferences – Chicago, San Francisco, and, of course, Boston. As a school that embraces democratic principles and actions, including student voice is important at Mission Hill.

Next week, staff will travel to Detroit for the annual meeting of the North Dakota Study Group. Middle school students Yimara Aponte Diaz, Ahsad Harvey, Alexa Lopez Ledesma, and

Jah'von Williams will be part of the travelling team. The title of this year's conference is "Build + Fight = Transformation? Building strategies and connections to fight for justice as we help solve the equation for transformed education."

The NDSG website, www.ndsg.org, is wonderful to explore: history, resources, videos, important statements and visions – your thinking about teaching, learning, and assessing, and participation in social change, will be provoked and enriched. To extend the "equation" metaphor, there are both variables and constants and a choice of operations (actions) involved in working towards a just solution. I'm glad we'll have the experience, vision, and voice of the kids with us when we gather in Detroit.

~Ann Ruggiero

Room 214
No news this week.

Hot Topics

Courtney's Corner
Check out Courtney's Corner for information on various programs and resources for you and your family.
Rincón de Courtney
Mira la información que esta fuera en el "Rincón de Courtney" para informatión sobre varios programas y recursos para ti y tu familia.

VOLUME 17, ISSUE 19   FEBRUARY 7, 2014

3rd Annual MHS Camp Night!
Mark your calendars for our upcoming Camp Night to be held Thursday, February 27th 6:30. Yes, it's already time to start thinking about camps. Camps are gearing up for summer and registration for many of them has already started! There will be representatives from different

camps both near and far for all ages. Something for everyone! Stop by and hear how to apply for financial aid or what transportation is available for the different camps. Don't see a camp there that you're interested in? Our website is also updated with many different programs and will continue to be updated throughout the rest of the year.

Fill out the Summer is Coming Survey online for Courtney if you'd like help getting programming for your child.

Turn in your Box Tops!
MHS is collecting Box Tops for Education all year long. You can drop off Box Tops at the Main Office, with Courtney in Room 114, or your child's classroom. Remember, each one is worth 10¢, so every one counts! Keep up the great work and turn them in when you clip them from products you use every day. Our next submission date is March 1, 2014, so turn them in **by February 24th** for them to count in this shipment. For a complete list of Box Tops products or to sign up online to

support our school, log onto www.boxtops4education.com.

Technology Tip - Common Sense Media
Did you know that our nation's children spend more time with media and digital activities than they do with their families or in school? As parent and teachers, it is incredibly difficult to keep up with the latest apps, games, websites, books, movies and more. How do we educate ourselves and help our children use technology in safe, healthy and age-appropriate ways? Common Sense Media (commonsensemedia.org) is my favorite website for trustworthy information – they are a non-profit organization proving reviews of new media, information on research, and Q&As/blog posts on relevant topics such as: "Sneaky Ways Advertisers Target Kids"; "Parents Guide to Kids and Cell Phones"; "Raising a Reader" and more. Common Sense Media is for parents of preschool children up trough teenagers. If you have questions about any of this – find me in Room 108 or email me at gmclaughlin@missionhillschool.org.
-Geralyn Bywater McLaughlin

Free February Fun

First Friday Open Studios
Friday, Feb 7 5:00p to 9:00p
More dates & times (10)
SOWA Artists Guild
Boston, MA
The First Friday of each month,

Guild member artists and others open their studios at 450 Harrison Ave. Boston, MA 02118. Meet the artists in their studios, see great art and buy directly from the artists. The SoWa Artists Guild strives to make art and artists accessible to everyone. Come and enjoy the fun. The event is free and parking is available.

Best of the Best -Ship Model show
USS Constitution Museum
Boston, MA
The USS Constitution Model Shipwright Guild and the USS Constitution Museum present the Best of the Best - 2014 Ship Model Show. Prize winning models from the past 10 annual shows will be featured, with over 100 handcrafted models of all sizes. Explore the intricate art of model. A visit to the Museum and the show is a great way for your family to spend the day.
Learn More -
http://www.ussconstitutionmuseum.org/exhibits/ship-model-show/

Family Gym - Blackstone
Saturday, Feb 8 10:00a to 11:30a
More dates & times (7)
BCYF Blackstone Community Center
Boston, MA
Looking for a free, fun way to be active with your kids? Drop by Family Gym, a play program for families with children ages 3-8 to get up, out and moving together. Family Gym takes place most Saturdays from 10:00-11:30 a.m. at BCYF's Blackstone Community Center in the South End. Family Gym is free and open to all, no pre-registration necessary. Children must be accompanied by an adult at all times.

President's Day Family Festival
Monday, Feb 17 11:00a to 3:00p
John F. Kennedy Presidential
Library and Museum
Boston, MA

Franklin Park Snow Festival
Saturday, Feb 8 1:00p to 4:00p
William J. Devine Golf Course
Boston, MA
Come sled, build snowpeople, track animal prints in the snow, try out snowshoes, or bring your own skis for a cross country park tour. You can warm up indoors with hot chocolate and board games. "Snow Day" - Saturday, February 22. There will be a winter hike in the woods if there's no snow. All ages welcome! Dress warmly and bring a sled if you have one, we'll have plenty to borrow for those without. Co-sponsored by the Boston Parks Department & Franklin Park Coalition.

3rd Annual Boston Storytelling Festival
Saturday, Feb 15, 9:30a to 4:30p
Boston Public Library - Central Branch: Boston Public Library, Rabb Lecture Hall
Boston, MA
Traditional storytelling in the morning , 21st century personal storytelling in the afternoon and 4-5 storytelling workshops happening all day long.

You don't want to miss this great opportunity to celebrate Storytelling as an art form.

Harvard Museum of Natural History: Massachusetts

residents are admitted free every Sunday morning from 9am to Noon year-round with proof of residency.

Free Admission Day at Museum of Fine Arts:
Saturday, February 8, 2014. Due to Lunar New Year, the MFA is free all day on Saturday! (Also, check out this event at the MFA in the afternoon!)

Chinatown Lion Dance Parade: Saturday, February 8, 2014. Enjoy this traditional celebration in Boston's Chinatown with lion dancers, traditional music, food, and more.

The Great Boston Couch Race: Saturday, February 8, 2014 from 11am to 5pm in the Prudential Center? Have you ever thought racing through an obstacle course on a couch would be cool? Well, you're in luck! Make sure to pre-register with a teammate if you're interested.

Free Thursdays at the ICA
Institute of Contemporary Art
http://www.icaboston.org/visit/hours-and-admission/
Every Thursday from 5 p.m. to 9 p.m., general admission to the Institute of Contemporary Art is free.

The Boston Public Library
will present free Black History Month Activities at many branch locations.
Feb. 10, 3:30 South End Branch, 685 Tremont Street

The Skin on My Chin:
Diversity Workshop For Children. In honor of Black History Month, Michelle Chalmers will read her fun, rhyming picture book, The Skin on My Chin, that explores diversity, ancestry and conversation about the skin. Children will learn about the sun and the diverse beauty of humanity. A fun craft is included. For Children 6 and up.

Feb. 11, 4:00 Grove Hall Branch, 41 Geneva Ave. Dorcheester
Boston musician Bill Lowe (trombonist and tubaist) will connect children
with Black History Month through music.
For Children ages 6-12

Free Tuesday Movies, 5:30 Mattapan Branch, 1350 Blue Hill Ave.
February 4 - The Wiz
February 11 - Ruby Bridges
February 18 - Princess & the Frog
February 25 - Akeelah and the Bee

About the Contributors

Katherine Clunis D'Andrea teaches 4-, 5-, and 6-year-olds at the Mission Hill School and is an adjunct professor at The University of Massachusetts Boston. A passionate schoolyard ecologist and environmental activist, Katherine has spent the past several years working with scientists and educators to help children and teachers deepen their understanding of science. She is also a self-proclaimed "playist," advocating for play-based education and the importance of children and families connecting with the outdoors. She is a change leader for Ashoka. When not in the classroom or schoolyard, Katherine is a passionate world traveler and has worked with children in the Caribbean, Africa, South America, and Europe. Katherine has been teaching for 17 years. She is the author of numerous articles, such as "Trust: A Master Teacher's Perspective on Why It Is Important. How to Build It and Its Implications for MBE Research" for *Mind, Brain and Education*, and "Tips for Helping Children Learn: The Three L's" for pbs.org. Katherine lives in Roxbury with her partner and son.

Emily Gasoi was a founding teacher at Mission Hill School who taught 2nd and 3rd grades and was coordinator of the Graduation by Portfolio process from 2002–2004. After working at Mission Hill School, Emily moved to Washington, DC, with her husband, Winston, where they adopted three cats and one child (in that order). She has worn many hats over the course of her 20-year career as an educator, including classroom teacher, curriculum and assessment developer, instructional coach, researcher, writer, and adjunct professor. In 2012 she earned a doctoral degree in Educational Leadership from the University of Pennsylvania. She currently works as a mentor for first-year teachers enrolled in the Inspired Teaching Teacher Training Program in Washington, DC.

Ayla Gavins left the small-town life of a Pennsylvania suburb at the age of 18 and moved to Boston to attend Boston University's School of Education. Upon graduation she began 6 years of teaching in two affluent suburbs of Boston. Her teaching career transitioned to Boston Public Schools where she taught ages 7 through 14 for 6 years at Mission Hill School. Under the guidance of Deborah Meier she received her school administrative license from the Principal Residency Network. She became principal of Mission Hill School in 2006. She has connected with a global audience of educators through presentations, conference participation, online presence, dialogue with school visitors, and writing.

Matthew Knoester is a National Board Certified Teacher and former teacher of 9- to 11-year-olds at Mission Hill School. He received his EdM from Harvard University and a PhD in curriculum and instruction from the University of Wisconsin–Madison, and is currently an assistant professor of education at the University of Evansville. He has written many articles focusing on literacy, social studies, and social contexts in education and is the author or editor of two previous books: *Democratic Education in Practice: Inside the Mission Hill School* (Teachers College Press, 2012) and *International Struggles for Critical Democratic Education* (Peter Lang, 2012), a recipient of the Critics' Choice Book Award from the American Educational Studies Association.

Heidi Lyne was one of the original teachers at Mission Hill. She was there for 10 years, first teaching 2nd and 3rd grades, then 6th, 7th, and 8th. She worked on the graduation requirements with the first two classes of 8th-graders and created a film and website about that process which can be found at www.goingpublicwithteaching.org/hlyne/. She is presently principal of the lower school at Neighborhood House Charter School in Boston.

Geralyn Bywater McLaughlin, MEd, has 25 years of experience in early childhood education and is the director of Defending the Early Years (DEYproject.org). She is an advocate for playful learning and works to support other teachers in becoming activists on behalf of young children. She is a founding teacher (and current early childhood teacher) at the Mission Hill School and the mother of twin boys who attend Mission Hill.

Deborah Meier began her work as a kindergarten teacher in Chicago and subsequently became the founding principal of four well-known public schools, including the Central Park East schools in New York and the Mission Hill School in Boston. She is the recipient of a 1987 MacArthur Fellowship "genius award" and has received honorary doctorates from many universities, including Harvard, Yale, and Dartmouth. She has written many essays and six previous books, including *The Power of Their Ideas: Lessons for America from a Small School in Harlem* (Beacon Press, 1995), *Can Standards Save Public Education?* (Beacon Press, 2000), *In Schools We Trust* (Beacon Press, 2002), *Keeping School: Letters to Families from Principals of Two Small Schools* (with Theodore R. Sizer and Nancy Faust Sizer, Beacon Press, 2004), *Many Children Left Behind: How the No Child Left Behind Act is Damaging*

Our Children and Our Schools (edited, with George Wood, Beacon Press, 2004), and *Playing for Keeps: Life and Learning on a Public School Playground* (with Brenda S. Engel and Beth Taylor, Teachers College Press, 2010). She blogs on the *Education Week* website at blogs.edweek.org/edweek/Bridging-Differences/ and on her homepage: deborahmeier.com.

Jeanne Rachko is entering her 18th year as a teacher at the Mission Hill School. She graduated from Massachusetts College of Art in 1983 with a degree in fine art, having studied photography, mixed media, music, movement, video, and film. Her earliest experience working with children (aside from a lot of babysitting, being from a family of seven children!) was in a preschool, where she became a lead teacher, certified by the state in early childhood education. She worked for almost 5 years with preschool-age children until she became pregnant and decided to stay home with her daughter and start a family care in her home until her daughter turned 5. Jeanne learned about Mission Hill School while looking for a school for her daughter. Upon first meeting Deborah Meier at an information session, Deborah asked Jeanne to send in a resume and the following year she started working in Mission Hill classrooms, first as an assistant teacher and eventually as the school's art teacher, where has been ever since. Her daughter, Brigita, attended Mission Hill from kindergarten through 8th grade.

Amy Valens began her teaching career as elementary art teacher in the public schools of Dayton, Ohio. After a year at Modern Playschool and Playmountain Place, an independent Summerhill-based school in Los Angeles, she returned to public schools in Northern California in 1974 when she became part of the Open Classroom of the Lagunitas School District. She held many positions there, finishing her career as the 3rd/4th-grade classroom teacher. Amy is the author of two children's books: *Jesse's Daycare* (Houghton Mifflin, 1990) and *Danilo the Fruit Man* (Dial, 1993). She retired from full-time teaching in June of 2006. Together with her husband, filmmaker Tom Valens, she has produced and directed *AUGUST TO JUNE: Bringing Life to School*, which followed her last class, and *Good Morning Mission Hill: The Freedom to Teach, the Freedom to Learn*, for which she was also the soundperson.

Tom Valens has been involved in film and video since the mid 1960s, working as a cameraman and editor for television news and documentary departments, for independent producers, and for himself. As editor, his films have won local and national Emmys as well as an Academy Award nomination. He filmed and edited *Nuclear Deception* (2005) for Helen Caldecott's Nuclear Policy Research Institute, and was second camera for Les Blank's much acclaimed *All in This Tea* (2007). His first film with his wife, Amy, *AUGUST TO JUNE: Bringing Life to School* (2011), has received much praise from parents and educators across the country. An earlier film about teaching, *To Make a Difference* (1985), was widely used by schools of education. *Good Morning Mission Hill* is the second use of the footage he shot at Mission Hill School, the first being the ten-part Internet series *A Year At Mission Hill*.

Jenerra Williams is a 14-year veteran at Mission Hill School and currently teaches 1st and 2nd grade. Before working at Mission Hill School, Jenerra had a variety of jobs, including working at Northeastern University at the John D. O'Bryant African-American Institute. It was there that her love of teaching and connecting with students was discovered. While obtaining her MEd through Northeastern, Jenerra was placed as a student intern at Mission Hill School. Her passion for teaching and making meaningful connections was a natural fit with the school's philosophy and approach to learning. Her work at Mission Hill has taken her across the country and internationally as well. From the hallways of the Capitol building to schools in Holland, sharing the work of Mission Hill School and what "good education" looks like has been an important part of her work as a teacher. Some organizations she is connected to outside of MHS are IDEA (Institute for Democratic Education in America), Ashoka, and Center for Teaching Quality.

Index

An *n* after a page number refers to an endnote.